Toymaker's Wooden Vehicles

PROJECTS & PLANS

Toymaker's Wooden Vehicles

PROJECTS & PLANS

Ralph S. Buckland

Sterling Publishing Co., Inc.   New York

Library of Congress Cataloging-in-Publication Data

Buckland, Ralph S.
  [Toymaker's book of wooden vehicles]
  Toymaker's wooden vehicles : projects and plans / Ralph S.
Buckland.
  p.   cm.
  Reprint. Originally published: The toymaker's book of wooden
vehicles. New York : Van Nostrand Reinhold, c1984.
  Bibliography: p.
  Includes index.
  ISBN 0-8069-6768-4 (pbk.)
  1. Wooden toy making.   2. Vehicles.   I. Title.
[TT174.5.W6B8   1988]
745.592—dc 19   87-29629
                                              CIP

        3   5   7   9   10   8   6   4   2

Published in 1988 by Sterling Publishing Co., Inc.
Two Park Avenue, New York, N.Y. 10016
Original edition published in hardcover by Van Nostrand Reinhold Company, Inc.
under the title "The Toymaker's Book of Wooden Vehicles"
© 1984 by Simon & Schuster, Inc.
Distributed in Canada by Oak Tree Press Ltd.
% Canadian Manda Group, P.O. Box 920, Station U
Toronto, Ontario, Canada M8Z 5P9
Distributed in the United Kingdom by Blandford Press
Link House, West Street, Poole, Dorset BH15 1LL, England
Distributed in Australia by Capricorn Ltd.
P.O. Box 665, Lane Cove, NSW 2066
Manufactured in the United States of America
All rights reserved
Sterling ISBN 0-8069-6768-4 Paper

Contents

For countless hours of transforming longhand notes into an accurately typed manuscript, constant encouragement, a willingness to work long weekends, vacations, and many, many, late nights, I thank and dedicate this book to my wife, Kathy.

Preface

Our technological world is increasingly giving humanity more leisure time. The age-old need to achieve with our hands as well as minds is common to both young and old persons. Whether the reader is a hobbyist, woodworker, teacher, or student, this book seeks to provide easy, understandable instructions, drawings, and helpful suggestions that will not only guide the reader in producing useful toys but will provide a rewarding and fulfilling experience in the completion of a project requiring hard work and skill.

Acknowledgments

Special thanks to my parents, Dr. Roscoe V. and Dorothy Buckland, whose guidance and understanding have given me the background and education necessary to make this book a reality.

I would like to express my appreciation to Nancy Green, Editor-in-Chief, Trade Books, Linda Venator, Managing Editor, Trade Books, and Laura J. Eisenstadt, Associate Editor, Trade Books, of Van Nostrand Reinhold Company, for their suggestions and help with the manuscript.

I would also like to thank photographer W. Weider of Canal Winchester, Ohio, for his suggestions and fine photography throughout the book.

A special thanks to Ken Saunders and Doug Osborn, two very fine teachers at the Groveport Madison Local School District, for their expertise and willingness to help with the manuscript.

PART ONE

INTRODUCTION TO WOODWORKING

Wood and Woodworking Techniques

Wood is our most plentiful and renewable natural resource. Its uses are infinite: our homes are constructed from wood, as is the furniture found in them. We often heat by wood, then sit and enjoy its warmth reading a newspaper, another wood product.

The hobbyist uses wood extensively, largely because it is easily worked. Its beauty, variations in color, and texture are unsurpassed by any other natural material. Working wood may require only a few hand tools; indeed, a skilled woodcarver may need only a pocket knife to produce lasting works of art. On the other hand, a craftsman may spend a lifetime collecting tools, machinery, and devices specifically designed for working wood.

Woodworking is a satisfying craft that may be pursued on a number of levels. Wood may be successfully worked with the simplest knowledge of wood and a basic understanding of tools. The professional craftsman may, however, spend a lifetime pursuing and mastering one special aspect of woodworking, developing knowledge and skills as a maker of fine furniture, a builder of harpsichords, a maker of fine guitars, a wood turner, a toymaker, or a carpenter. You can explore woodworking at whatever level you feel most comfortable, creating whatever objects you wish. You need not be a skilled artisan to enjoy the satisfaction of working with wood.

TYPES OF WOOD

Wood can be divided into two basic categories, hardwoods and softwoods. Some examples of common hardwoods used for toys, crafts, and furniture include oak, cherry, walnut, maple, chestnut, mahogany, poplar, birch, ash, and hickory. The term hardwood does not refer to the physical hardness of the wood. Rather, hardwoods are classified as those trees with broad leaves, which often bear fruit or nuts. An example of a hardwood that is physically soft is balsa, a wood used extensively in making model airplanes.

Softwoods are from trees that have needles, such as the evergreens. They include the pines, redwoods, cypresses, cedars, hemlocks, and spruces. Although called soft, their texture is sometimes harder than the hardwoods; for example, white pine is very similar in physical hardness to poplar, yet white pine is a softwood and poplar is a hardwood.

Softwoods are recommended for toys for several reasons. People often overlook the beauty and excellent working characteristics of common softwood lumber, such as the woods used for home construction. Generally speaking, the softwoods are less expensive than the hardwoods. Beginners almost always make mistakes: making mistakes on a hard-to-find hardwood, which may cost five to ten times as much as an equivalent piece of softwood, may be very frustrating because it is expensive. Scrap softwood lumber from building sites often can be obtained for the asking. When a home is built, rafters or floor joists are often cut off, leaving short scrap pieces that are usually thrown away. The pieces may be as short as a foot, but this is ample material to build a truck, tractor, or almost any of the toys shown in this book.

Softwoods are also usually physically softer, and thus safer for toys than are hardwoods. A child playing with a wooden truck, for example, may drop it on his toe. A softwood toy would probably cause less injury than the same toy made from a hardwood. Hardwoods offer a wide selection of colors and textures. In general they are stronger and heavier. Hardwoods generally require sharper tools and more work time. A handy hardwood supplier is not always located in the immediate neighborhood, but almost any building supply store, lumber company, or hardware store handles softwoods and the materials required for the toys described in this book.

Throughout the book dowel rods and 1⅜-inch round molding appear in the materials lists. Dowel rods are round pieces of hardwood usually bought in pieces 3 to 4 feet long. They rang in size from ¼ inch up to 1 inch in diameter. Sizes larger than this are not very common. For this reason 1⅜-inch-diameter round molding is also recommended. It is round like a dowel but made of softwood. These moldings are easy to find in almost any lumber company or building supply store. Dowel rods and round moldings eliminate the necessity of using a wood lathe to build many of the toys, although round stock could easily be turned to the proper diameter on a wood lathe.

BUYING LUMBER

Softwood may be purchased at almost any lumber company that sells lumber for residential construction. Softwoods are normally sold in standard sizes, such as a 1-by-6-inch piece of stock, which is actually ¾ inch thick by 5⅝ inches wide. The size 1 by 6 inches is the approximate size of lumber you pay for before the board is planed smooth. A 2-by-4-inch piece of stock is actually 1⅝ by 3⅝ inches. Softwoods are generally bought in standard lengths ranging from 8 to 20 feet, in two foot intervals.

Hardwoods are handled by specialty lumber companies. They are sold in a rough form and must be planed smooth. Some lumber companies will plane lumber to specific sizes for an additional fee. Hardwoods are generally sold by the board foot. One board foot is 12 inches wide by 12 inches long by 1 inch thick, or 144 cubic inches. When you purchase a 1-inch-thick piece of hardwood, it *is* actually 1 inch thick but must be planed and smoothed to a workable size.

Hardwoods and softwoods may be warped, cupped, split, or checked. Defects such as warped or cupped boards may be difficult to work and also dangerous because they may cause kickback on machines like a table saw or radial arm saw. Splits and checks are dangerous when doing lathe work and should be avoided. When purchasing lumber, try to be selective and avoid unwanted defects.

Generally speaking, buy enough lumber to make all the parts on a toy's parts list. Estimate some extra material for waste if unwanted defects are present and for a few wasteful mistakes that even a skilled craftsman sometimes makes. Some lumber will need to be resawed or planed to a thinner size. If you choose not to do your own resawing, have a professional help plane the stock to its required thickness at the lumberyard.

WOOD-WORKING SAFETY

Working with wood can be a satisfying, enjoyable experience, but lack of seriousness and awareness of safety can be disastrous. Power tools can quickly produce fascinating and beautiful objects, but before operating any machine you should understand how it functions and the possible mistakes you could make. Consult the manufacturer's guide or an indepth text on woodworking and do some serious study before operating power equipment. Personal instruction from an experienced professional is strongly recommended. You should also learn about hand tools before using them. The wood chisel, for example, can be a very dangerous tool if used incorrectly; when used correctly, it rarely causes accidents.

Keep in mind that the shop may be interesting to others and may attract innocent curiosity seekers. Children and pets should not be allowed in the workshop area. Some of the following suggestions may help prevent accidents.

1. Keep all power equipment locked when not in use.
2. Do not leave protruding nails in boards; someone could step on them.
3. Keep floors clean; sawdust can be very slippery.
4. Keep tools stored in a well-organized manner, not hanging over table edges or lying on the floor.
5. When using a wood chisel, use a vise or clamp, not your hand, to hold the wood.
6. Always wear safety glasses, even when working with hand tools. The glasses provide protection from flying wood chips.
7. Push away from your body when using a knife or wood chisel.
8. Turn power tools off before making adjustments.
9. Do not wear loose clothing or jewelry that may become entangled in moving parts of machinery.
10. Remove rings before operating equipment. Rings may get caught in moving parts and shear off a finger.
11. Keep fingers and hands away from the cutting edge of tools.
12. Never talk to or interrupt anyone who is working on a machine or turn your attention from the machine while you are working on it. Keep your eyes focused on the cutting action at all times.
13. Be sure wood chisels, files, awls, hammers, and mallets have handles that are secure

14. Keep all tools in good repair. Do not allow cutting edges to become dull.
15. Use the correct tool for the job; for example, do not use a chisel for driving screws.
16. Never run in the workshop.
17. Do not carry more tools than you can handle safely.
18. Use good common sense and always consider the safety of others.

WOOD-WORKING HARDWARE

Wood Screws

Wood screws are used to fasten boards together. They hold better and longer than nails. Wood screws also allow you to take pieces apart easily, whereas pulling apart nailed stock may be difficult without damaging the boards.

Wood screws used in woodworking usually have slotted heads or Phillip's heads. Phillip's head screws have 2 slots crossing at 90-degree angles.

A variety of shapes is available for the heads of a screw. The flat head is used when the screw top should be flush with the board. When measuring a flat head screw, the head is included in the length of the screw.

The entire head of the round head screw protrudes above the board. The head is not included in its length measurement; only the part that penetrates the wood is measured.

The oval head screw is a cross

between the flat head and round head screws in that part of its head lies above the wood surface and part below. Its length is considered to be that part of the screw that penetrates the board.

Wood screw sizes are determined by two factors. First, the largest diameter of the screw shank is given in gauge sizes. A number 0 gauge is 1/16 inch in diameter; a number 30 gauge is 7/16 inch in diameter. The screws used in this book for toymaking are number 8 (11/64 inch) or 10 (13/64 inch).

The second factor determining screw size is the screw length, that is, that part that goes into the wood. Screw lengths commonly vary from 3/8 to 4 inches.

Holes are often drilled in a board before a wood screw is inserted to keep the board from cracking as the screw is driven into it. This also makes driving the screw much easier.

Use a drill bit designed to match the screw shape, sometimes called a combination wood screw and countersink. These drill bits match the size of a screw. For example, a number 10 gauge by 1¼ inches long screw would require a number 10 by 1¼ inches long combination drill and countersink. These bits were used on the toys throughout this book.

Nails

Almost everyone has at one time or another used nails. Nails provide a quick and easy way to attach or join two pieces of wood. Nails are commonly used in rough carpentry for framing houses, as well as for finishing work, including framing around doors and windows; they are also frequently used in cabinet-making. Nails are not used in

building fine furniture, where skillfully made joints connect the parts. Small nails and brads are excellent for use in toymaking.

Nails can be bought in a large variety of sizes and shapes. The size of a nail is described by the term penny, often abbreviated *d*, which indicates the length of the nail. Sizes range from a 2-penny to a 60-penny nail. For example, a 2*d* nail is a 2-penny nail, about 1 inch long. The *d* also indicates the weight of a thousand nails to a pound: one thousand 2-penny nails weigh 2 pounds. The length of a 4-penny nail is about 1½ inches, a 6-penny nail is about 2 inches long, and a 10-penny nail is roughly 3 inches long.

There are many kinds of nails designed for a variety of jobs. The "common nail" is a thick nail with a thick head. It is used in rough carpentry when the frame of a home is being constructed. These nails are commonly used for almost any kind of construction where the boards are of a 2- by 4-inch size or larger.

Box nails have a thin, flat head and are thinner in diameter than a common nail.

The finishing nail is used extensively by the carpenter doing finishing work, because these

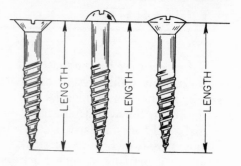

FLAT HEAD WOOD SCREW ROUND HEAD WOOD SCREW OVAL HEAD WOOD SCREW

nails can be easily concealed. The finishing nail can be countersunk using a nailset and covered up easily and quickly with wood filler. Finishing nails are used extensively on the toy projects shown in this book.

Brads, small nails with rounded heads, are ¼ to 1½ inches long. They are often sold in a gold or brass color as well as the standard silver. These nails are very thin and generally are used in softwoods. If wire brads were driven into a hard piece of wood, like maple, oak, or cherry, they would probably bend; pre-drill holes for brads when using them in hardwoods. On the other hand, a soft piece of wood like white pine will not damage brads. The brad is an excellent way of joining small parts in softwoods, particularly the many parts of the toys found in this book.

Almost everyone has driven nails. The common claw hammer may be bought in a variety of sizes for different nailing operations. When using small nails such as wire brads or small finishing nails, select a light hammer—a 13-ounce hammer is recommended.

Nails often have to be pulled for a variety of reasons. The claws of a hammer are designed for pulling nails. When larger nails are to be pulled, as in framing work, a crowbar should be used to provide more leverage than the common claw hammer can.

Finishing nails, once countersunk, may be difficult to remove without damage to the board. Driving the nail's head back through the board is sometimes possible. If this is not the case, take a wood chisel and carve away enough wood to grip the nail's head with a pair of needle nose pliers.

GLUING AND CLAMPING

Polyvinyl (white) and aliphatic resin glue are ready-to-use glues. They are very strong when used with wood; for best results the parts should be clamped. Only these glues were used on the toys in this book. They can be found in almost any hardware, lumber, or building-supply store.

Clamping pieces of wood will ensure a tighter-fitting joint and increase strength over a non-clamped joint. Nailing and clamping are suggested throughout this book, nails being used on smaller pieces instead of clamps. By nailing, you do not have to wait for the glue to dry, only to clamp another joint and wait again. The nails hold the pieces while the glue dries. Nails are also less awkward than clamps, especially on small toys.

Three types of clamps are useful in any type of woodworking: the bar or cabinetmakers clamp, the C-clamp, and the hand screw. The toymaker may need only a C-clamp and hand screw, since the long bar clamps are mainly for larger projects.

Pregluing Hints

Before you apply any glue, be sure you have enough clamps to successfully hold the boards being glued. Applying the glue over several pieces of stock only to find out you do not have enough clamps can be a frustrating experience. Gluing without proper clamps creates a weak joint. Regluing and reclamping involve removing the old glue, a messy and wasteful procedure.

The surfaces or edges being glued should be planed or surfaced smooth and should be flat. The surfaces should match or lie against each other without any gaps between them. Parts to be glued should also be free of dust, grease, or dirt. When gluing on something other than a glue table (a metal-topped table from which the dried glue can easily be scraped), lay out paper to protect the table surface. If the glue drips on the table and hardens, it may be difficult to remove without damaging the table surface.

Most glues work best at a specified temperature. Check the manufacturer's recommendations and be sure the room temperature is within the correct limits.

When clamping wood parts, a small scrap block of a very soft wood (pine is excellent) between the clamp and the project will prevent the clamp from denting the project when the clamp is tightened.

Applying the Glue

Spread a thin, evenly distributed layer of glue on the surfaces using a brush, stick, or your hand. Most glues used for woodworking are easily washed off with water when they are still wet. See the manufacturer's suggestions for clean-up solutions. Be sure there are no areas without glue.

Space clamps equally around the boards and tighten them a little at a time. Tighten one clamp slightly, then move to the others; repeat this until all the clamps are tight. This alternating process will equalize pressure on the joint. Glue should be squeezed out along all of the joints, leaving no cracks between the glued boards. Removing the excess glue immediately will save time in the long run, since the

6

excess glue will harden and will have to be removed by scraping or using a wood chisel.

Allow the glue to dry for the time the manufacturer recommends before removing the clamps. The glued joint should be as strong as the wood itself and the pieces that have been glued may be worked as one piece of wood without concern that the parts will separate. Glued (laminated) wood can be turned, sawed, jointed, and even planed. Special effects using woods of different colors and grain patterns are often created by gluing.

FINISHING

Finishing a toy may be as simple as spraying it with an inexpensive can of spray lacquer or may involve the use of sophisticated spraying equipment or hours of hand rubbing an oil finish. Regardless of the selection of a finish, the surfaces must first be prepared to accept the finish. Defects such as knot holes, cracks, and nail holes must be concealed. Imperfections or undesired surfaces may be covered quickly by using a variety of wood fillers. Many times the effect of a knot or other defect may enhance the beauty and give the project its own personality—covering all defects is not necessarily advisable.

Plastic Wood is a wood filler available in a can or tube; it may be applied with a knife, putty knife, or wood chisel. Plastic Wood hardens quickly and may be sanded to a smooth finish. Several applications of Plastic Wood may be required since it shrinks slightly as it dries, causing slight depressions. Be sure to read the manufacturer's recommendations for applying the fin-

ish. Plastic Wood is available in many colors to match various stains.

Stick Shellac is another commonly used filler and may be obtained from any good woodworking supplier. Stick Shellac may be purchased in a large variety of colors. To apply Stick Shellac, it must be melted with a soldering iron or soldering gun and allowed to flow into the defect. When allowed to cool, Stick Shellac regains its original hardness. Some sanding will probably be required.

Filler sticks of soft plastic, which can easily be applied with a knife, are also available. Filler sticks stay soft, do not shrink, and can be purchased in a large variety of colors. Filler sticks can be obtained from almost any hardware or lumber company.

After you have corrected the defects to your satisfaction the next step in the finishing process is the final sanding. Three types of sandpaper are available. Flint sandpaper, made from flint or quartz, is the least expensive and is usually sold in grit grades of fine, medium, and coarse. Garnet sandpaper, usually reddish in color, is a better quality of sandpaper and will outlast flint paper. Aluminum oxide sandpaper will outlast flint and garnet sandpaper but is even more expensive.

Always sand with the grain to prevent deep harsh cuts and scratches in the wood. Start sanding with a medium or coarse paper, depending on the surface condition. Work down to the finer grades until a suitably smooth surface is reached. After the project has been sanded properly, apply the finish.

In this book both oil finishes and sprayed lacquer finishes have been used. Oil finishes provide a low-luster finish when rubbed on in one or two coats in small

amounts; for deeper effects the finish may require as many as ten or more coats and hours of rubbing. Raw linseed oil was used for most of the projects in this book. Apply linseed oil with a cloth, leaving a thin coat. Linseed oil may require as long as a week to dry completely. Dispose of the cloths used to apply linseed oil since spontaneous combustion may occur. Linseed oil leaves a penetrating finish that is tough and lasting. A little linseed oil will go a long way and is easily applied. Tung oil, Danish oil, and Watco oil are also easily applied and will seal and finish toys to a flat natural appearance.

Spray lacquer is inexpensive and is bought in a spray can. Spray lacquers are easy to apply and usually provide a glossy finish. For those wishing to finish toys in quantity, spray equipment may be used for spraying lacquer. Lacquers may also be applied with a brush. Regardless of the method of application, lacquer dries quickly and leaves a beautiful finish when applied properly.

Many synthetic resins that produce clear finishes are available: polyurethane, spar varnish, and Deft.

Wood stains are available in a wide range of colors and with proper use may enhance the beauty of the project. The use of paint to finish wooden toys detracts from the natural beauty of the wood.

The toys in this book were finished after they were completely assembled. After any finish has dried, a coat of furniture wax will protect the finish and further enhance the beauty of the toy.

Woodworking Tools and Equipment

The basic woodworking tools have undergone few changes since early settlers used them. Once the knowledge and skill to use them correctly are acquired, they may be employed in many areas. Toymaking is only one area of woodworking; the same tools are valuable and essential in woodworking's many other facets. Making toys may require only a few choice hand tools. But as your skills and interests increase you may wish to purchase more tools. Most well-equipped home shops are a result of many years of learning and investing. High-quality tools are a good investment, both materially and in the pride and satisfaction one receives by using them.

The most common woodworking hand tools and power equipment are described below. Keep in mind that only a few may be required for any one toy.

HAND TOOLS

Layout Tools

Try Square: Try squares are used as layout and measurement tools to draw lines at 90 degrees or, with some try squares, 45 degrees. They are frequently used to check a project to see if the parts are square. Some of the newer try squares have both metric and standard scales stamped on the blade and are divided into eighths or sixteenths of an inch. Try squares range in size from 6 to 12 inches long.

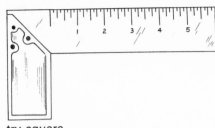
try square

Framing Square: This tool is frequently used by carpenters to lay out (draw) the angles of roof rafters and the notches in the boards used for steps. It is also useful in toymaking as a layout and measurement tool when working with large material, such as plywood.

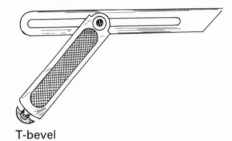
T-bevel

T-bevel: The T-bevel is used to transfer an angle from one location to another. When used with a protractor an angle can be measured with a T-bevel.

Flexible Steel Rule: These rules are especially useful for layout work on large parts such as a full 4- by 8-foot sheet of plywood. They range in size from a small 12 inch metal rule to more than 100 feet.

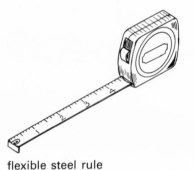
flexible steel rule

Marking Gauge: This tool is a must for laying out parallel lines or lines parallel to an edge. The marking gauge uses a sharp point to scribe a parallel line as it is pulled along the edge of a board.

marking gauge

Tramble Points: Often in woodworking you will need to construct large circles. Most compasses will draw a circle of only about 12 inches in diameter. Tramble points are two sharp-pointed, steel shafts (similar to those on dividers) that can be fastened to a small piece of wood. The wood, of any practi-

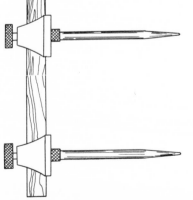
tramble points

cal length, thus becomes a large compass. Circles as large as 20 feet in diameter can easily be made using tramble points.

Divider: Dividers are similar to compasses except that one leg scratches a line instead of a mark with a piece of lead or pencil. They are used for layout work, to draw arcs or circles.

Saws

Crosscut Saw: Crosscut saws are designed to cut across the grain of a piece of wood at 90 degrees. Crosscut saws have knife-like teeth: every other tooth is bent to one side. They vary from 20 to 26 inches in length. Common saws have 8 to 10 teeth per inch.

Ripsaw: Ripsaws are used to cut with the grain or in the same direction as the grain. They can be bought in sizes of 20 to 28 inches long. They usually have 5 to 7 teeth per inch. The ripsaw teeth are flat on the bottom and cut in fashion similar to the wood chisel.

Back Saw: This saw gets its name because it has a hard and rigid back. It has small, fine, crosscut teeth, which enable it to cut very smoothly. Back saws are used where precision is a necessity, such as in cutting joints for fine furniture. The saw that is used in a miter box and is called a "miter box saw" is really a back saw.

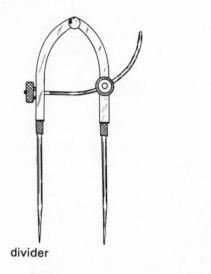

divider

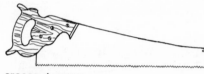

crosscut saw

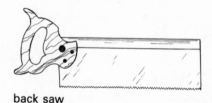

back saw

Dovetail Saw: The dovetail saw gets its name from its use as the prime hand tool used to cut dovetail joints (a joint used commonly in the drawers of fine furniture). It has extremely fine crosscut teeth, finer than a back saw, and produces a very fine finished cut.

Coping Saw: This type of hand saw is used to cut curves in stock that is less than ¾ inch thick. The blade can be removed and inserted through a hole in the board to be cut, then remounted on the coping saw frame to make inside cuts to that board.

Miter Box Saw: This piece of equipment is used to cut angles on a piece of wood. It may be set at any angle, although 90-, 45-, and 22½-degree angles are the most commonly used. Miter boxes may simply be made of a piece of wood and a back saw. More expensive models are made of metal; the most efficient miter box is electric.

Hacksaw: Often in woodworking it may be necessary to cut a piece of metal. Hacksaws can cut through almost any kind of soft metal, although cutting tool steel or a harder piece of steel would be difficult. The teeth on the hacksaw should point away from the handle. A variety of types and sizes of hacksaw blades may be purchased. Store clerks may give professional advice concerning the correct blade required for a particular job.

dovetail saw

Planes

Jack Plane: This plane may be used to straighten a curved edge on a board and to produce a smooth, square edge. Jack planes, approximately 14 inches long, are the most commonly used of all planes.

jack plane

Smooth Plane: This plane is similar in construction and parts to the jack plane but is shorter, usually 8 inches in length. It is used to produce a smooth, straight surface on the edge or face of a board.

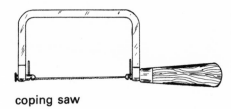

coping saw

Block Plane: This tool is especially designed for planing the end off a board or small piece of wood. It is usually about 6 inches long.

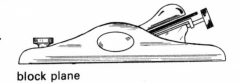

block plane

Chisels, Files, Knives

Wood Files: These tools are available in a wide range of textures, ranging from a smooth-cutting to a faster, rough-cutting file. They are used in sculpting, shaping, and forming wood. They also are frequently used to smooth a rough surface. Common shapes of files are round, half round, flat, and triangular.

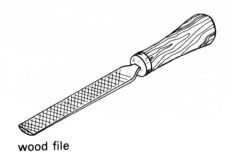

wood file

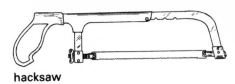

hacksaw

File Card: Files often become clogged with wood fibers and thus lose their effectiveness. A file card is a wire brush that is used to clean clogged wood fibers out of the file's cutting edges. Some file cards have a bristle brush on them as well as the wire brush.

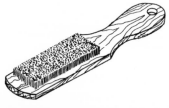

file card

Rasp: A rasp is used for rough forming and has larger teeth than a file. Rasps are also available in round, half round, flat, and triangular shapes.

Putty Knife: A putty knife has a handle similar to that of a wood chisel. Its blade is a blunt, flat piece of metal. It gets its name from being used to press putty around windows. These knives are very useful when pressing wood filler into nail holes or patching other defects.

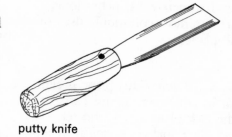

putty knife

Utility Knife: These knives are also called razor blade knives and are often used in opening cardboard boxes. They are extremely sharp, and their large handles make them fairly safe, but caution must be used. As a woodworking tool they are handy for carving and for jobs requiring fine cuts.

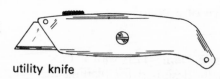

utility knife

Scraper Blade: A scraper blade is used to remove irregularities in the surface of a piece of wood. These defects may be caused by the planing process or incorrect use of a jointer. It is also a useful tool for removing excess glue from the surface of boards. Imperfections may be scraped out easily with a scraper blade, which is quicker than sanding. The blades are usually rectangular in shape, although some have curved edges. They should be sharpened on their scraping edge.

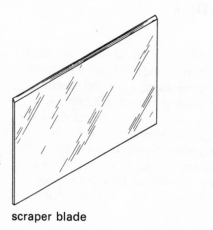

scraper blade

Wood Chisel: Wood chisels have many uses in many types of woodworking. A good general safety rule for using chisels is to keep both hands on the chisel. Use a clamp to secure the stock

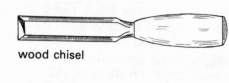

wood chisel

when carving. Do not try to hold the stock with one hand and the chisel with the other: doing this invites an accident. A mallet can be used to strike a chisel for deeper cuts but a hammer should not be used as it will eventually ruin the handle of a chisel, especially if the handle is metal or plastic. Chisel sizes are established by the width of their blade. They vary in size from ¼ to 2 inches.

Modern chisels are attached to their handles in two ways: the socket chisel has a handle that is forced into a cone-shaped cavity; the tang chisel, which has a tapered end much like the end of a file, is wedged into the handle.

Several kinds of chisels are available for a variety of tasks. The firmer chisel has a thick blade and is used for general purpose work. The paring chisel, which usually has a tang handle and a thin blade with beveled sides, is used for fine cutting. A butt chisel has a shorter blade than the paring or firming chisel; it is the most commonly used woodworking chisel. The butt chisel is used commonly in furniture making and fine woodworking. A mortise chisel is designed to cut the mortise (hole) part of a mortise-and-tenon joint. A gouge is a chisel with a cupshaped blade used commonly by woodcarvers to make a curved cut. Many special shapes of chisels are available for a variety of jobs. Some woodcarvers even grind their own chisels.

Drills and Drill Bits

Awl: An awl is a punch with a wooden or plastic handle. An essential tool in every workshop, it is used to punch holes to start screws or drill bits.

Auger Bit: These bits should be used only with a hand brace. They cannot be used safely in a drill press, since the end, or tang, of the auger bit is square shaped. Common auger bit sizes range from ¼ to 1 inch in diameter.

Twist Bit: The most common type of drill bit is the twist bit, which can drill holes in wood and metal. These bits may be purchased in common sizes from ¹⁄₁₆ to 1 inch in diameter. Larger sizes are available but are usually found only in machine shops where very large drill presses are used. When making wooden toys, these drill bits are used in drill presses or electric drills.

Spade Bit: Spade or power bits are flat and are used to drill holes in wood with electric drills or drill presses. They range in size from ¼ to 2 inches.

Forstner Bit: One of the few drill bits that drill a hole with a flat bottom, the Forstner bit is not tapered or pointed on its end. Many of the wheels in this book were made using a Forstner bit.

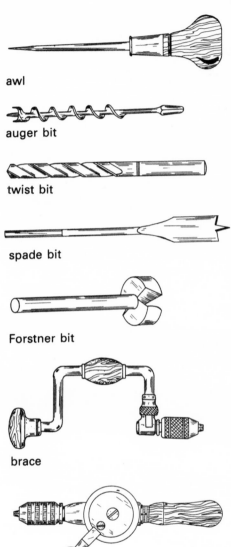

awl

auger bit

twist bit

spade bit

Forstner bit

brace

hand drill

Brace: A brace is a device commonly used to hold an auger bit when drilling holes ranging in size from ¼ to 2 inches in diameter. The brace can also hold other types of tools, such as screwdriver bits, for quickly and efficiently driving a screw; expansion bits, which adjust to the size of the hole being drilled; and countersink bits, which cut 60-degree holes for the head part of a flat head screw to fit in.

Hand Drill: This tool should not be confused with an electric hand drill. The hand drill is a much overlooked tool, providing very efficient means of drilling small holes, less than ¼ inch, in wood or metal without electricity. The hand drill uses twist bits.

Combination Wood Drill and Countersink: This drill bit does two jobs in one operation. It drills a pilot hole for the shank of the screw and also drills a countersink hole for the head of a flat head screw.

Plug Cutter: A plug cutter cuts a plug to cover the head of a sunken flat head screw. These plugs are often used on furniture to cover unsightly screws and give the appearance of a joint being held together by pegs or dowels.

Clamps

Bar Clamp: Sometimes called a cabinetmakers clamp because of its common use in furniture or cabinetmaking shops, this clamp is used to hold a number of boards together, such as in a tabletop. Bar clamps range in size from 1 to 6 feet long. In early American furniture shops, they were made of wood but today are commonly made of steel, pipe, or plastic.

C-clamp: The C-clamp gets its name from its resemblance to the letter C. Most often made of steel, it is used to clamp small pieces of wood. The size of a C-clamp is determined by the largest piece of stock that it can hold or clamp. Common sizes range from a 1-inch to a 6-inch opening.

Hand Screw: This common tool was found in early American woodworking shops. It was once made entirely of wood, including wooden screw threads. Today, however, the threads are steel and the jaws of the clamps are wood or plastic. These clamps are very useful in clamping small objects.

Hammers and Mallets

Mallets: Several kinds of mallets are available. The rubber mallet with a rubber head is commonly used in gluing operations, when there is a need to tap or force a joint together without putting marks or dents in the wood. Wood and leather mallets are fre-

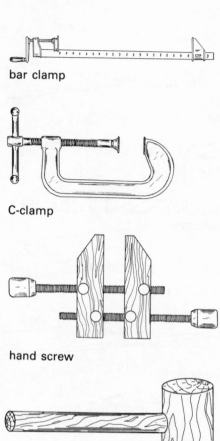

bar clamp

C-clamp

hand screw

mallet

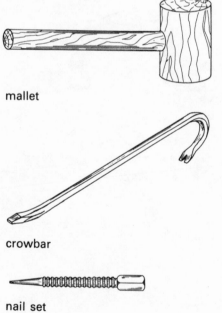

crowbar

nail set

quently used to strike wood chisels and wood carving tools.

Crowbar: Crowbars, sometimes called wrecking bars, are useful in pulling nails that cannot easily be pulled with a claw hammer. The handle is longer than that of a hammer, providing more leverage and thus more pulling power on the nail. They are made of steel.

Claw Hammer: The claw hammer, usually 16 ounces, is used for pulling and driving nails. A smaller 13-ounce size is ideal for driving small brads; it is also a good size for young woodworkers.

Nail Set: These are used to countersink a nail, that is, to drive it below the surface. Nail sets are mostly used with finishing nails. They may be obtained in several sizes to match the nail size being used.

Screwdrivers

Phillip's Screwdriver: The Phillip's screwdriver is used with the Phillip's head screw, which has two adjacent, right-angle slots.

Standard Screwdriver: Standard screwdrivers are used with the common single-slotted screw.

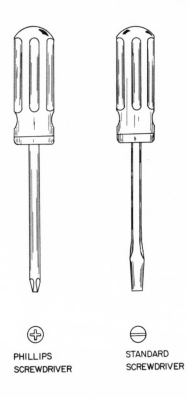

PHILLIPS
SCREWDRIVER

STANDARD
SCREWDRIVER

Vise: A woodworker vise attaches to a shop bench and is used to hold stock, leaving both hands free to work.

Miscellaneous Hand Tools

Pliers: Pliers are used to get a better grip on an object than could be provided by the hand. They often have wire cutters on them and may be bought in a variety of shapes and sizes. Needle nose pliers have a long, narrow, gripping jaw, ideal for grasping small objects, such as brads. Slip joint pliers may be adjusted to various sizes.

Chuck Key: This device is used to loosen or tighten a chuck. A chuck is the holding mechanism on a drill press or an electric hand drill that holds the bit. The chuck key should always be removed from the chuck before the drill or drill press is allowed to start. If left in the drill, it could be thrown, causing an accident.

NEEDLE NOSE PLIERS

SLIP JOINT PLIERS

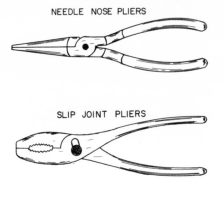

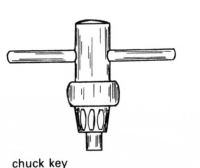

chuck key

WOOD-WORKING MACHINES

Jigsaw: The jigsaw is used to cut curves. It can be used easily with boards as thick as 2 inches. The size of a jigsaw is determined by the distance from the blade to the back frame of the saw. Common sizes range from 18 to 24 inches. Jigsaws are very safe and are therefore preferable over band saws for teaching a beginner to cut a curve. A beginner's mistake on the jigsaw may cause a minor cut, whereas the same mistake on a band saw may mean the loss of a finger. Jigsaws can be equipped with a variety of blades, ranging from the fast-cutting larger-toothed blades (1/4 inch wide) to the smooth-cutting fine blades, some of which are only approximately 1/16 inch wide.

Lathe: The lathe is the oldest type of power woodworking equipment. It is used to form cylindrical shapes such as dowels. Lathes are also designed to cut metal and are often used for cutting plastic and other materials. The wood lathe is essential for building furniture and is often used in other kinds of woodworking. In this book the lathe was used in making the steam engine, both tankers, the grader, the tractor, the earthmover, and the road roller. Some craftsmen spend a lifetime learning and perfecting their skills doing wood turning, or lathe work.

Jointer: The jointer is an electrically powered machine designed to straighten the edge or face of a board and at the same time make it smooth. This smooth edge can be cut from a 45- to a 90-degree angle. The jointer performs basically the same operations as a hand plane. The size of a jointer is determined by the length of the jointer knives (blades). Thus a 4-inch jointer could joint a board up to 4 inches wide. The 4- and 6-inch jointers are common for home use; school and industry may have jointers up to 16 inches in size.

Planer: Planers, sometimes called surfacers or thickness planers, not only smooth the face of a board as a jointer does, but also make it parallel to its opposite surface. Planers are rarely found in home workshops because of their high cost. Schools and wood-related industries find planers a necessity because of the large volume and variety of thicknesses required on the various projects and products being made.

Drill Press: Drill presses may be used with metals and plastic as well as with wood. Their most common use is for drilling holes. Like many other types of power equipment, special attachments can be secured for sanding, cutting holes, shaping fancy edges, mortising (a process that cuts a square hole used mainly in the mortise-and-tenon joint found commonly in fine furniture construction), and other advanced operations. The size of a drill press is determined by the distance from the center of the chuck to the back frame or column. Drill presses for home use may range in size from 8 to 20

inches. A factor to consider in buying a drill press is its chuck size. A ½-inch chuck could hold up to a ½-inch diameter drill bit, a very practical size for home use. Other common sizes of chucks for home and school are ¼ and ⅜ inch. Larger chuck sizes, necessary in industry, require large drill presses and are very expensive.

Electric Drill: The portable and lightweight electric hand drill is a popular tool for home, school, and commercial use. The common sizes of chucks available are ¼, ⅜, and ½ inch. In this book the twist bit, spade bit, Forstner bit, plug cutter, and combination wood drill and countersink are used extensively in an electric hand drill.

Hole Saw: The hole saw is used by carpenters to cut the round holes used to fit a lock in a door. Hole saws are used throughout this book for making wheels. The waste portion (the center piece of wood) of the stock is used for the wheels. The blades on most hole saws can be changed to various diameters. Common sizes range from 1 to 3 inches in diameter. When used to make wheels, a drill press is recommended, although it is not a necessity. The more expensive hole saws have a hexagonal (six-sided) shaft, which will not slip in the drill's chuck as easily as the round shaft.

Radial Arm Saw: The radial arm saw gets its name from the arm that extends out over the table and can be rotated 360 degrees. The blade, attached directly to the motor, can be rotated to any desired angle. This saw is some-

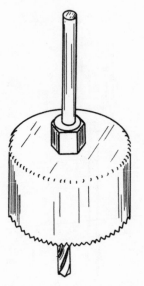

Hole saw

times called a cutoff saw because it was originally used for crosscutting or cutting boards to desired lengths. It may be used for crosscutting (cutting across the grain) and ripping (cutting with the grain). Special blades or attachments can be bought for the radial arm to cut fancy moldings or grooves and for sanding. Most radial arm saws for home use are 8 or 10 inches in size, determined by the largest blade diameter that the saw is designed to accommodate.

Table Saw: The table saw, sometimes referred to as a circular or bench saw is used mainly to rip or crosscut boards. The size of a table saw is determined by the diameter of the largest blade it will accommodate: a table saw capable of using a blade 10 inches in diameter is referred to as a 10-inch table saw. Most saws designed for home use are 8- or 10-inch saws. Schools and industries often have 12-, 14-, and 16-inch table saws.

Band Saw: Band saws get their name from their circular, flexible, steel blade. The blade is one continuous piece of metal with teeth in it. The blade revolves around two wheels, one at the top, the other at the bottom of the machine. The diameter of these wheels determine the size of the band saw: a band saw with a 10-inch diameter wheel would be called a 10-inch band saw. Common sizes of band saws range from a small 10-inch saw made for home use to the larger saws found in industry that reach 30 inches.

Band saws quickly and efficiently cut curves and straight cuts in stock often as thick as 4 to 6 inches, more on larger models. Generally the band saw blade is wider than that of a jigsaw and thus cannot cut the sharp curves and detailed scroll work commonly done by jigsaws. Since the band saw blade has no end the band saw cannot make inside cuts.

When cutting stock 2 or more inches thick, a large portion of the blade is exposed after each cut. A slip or misguided hand can easily result in the loss of a finger (or a hand) because of the band saw's fast cutting action.

The skills required for band saw operations are very similar to those used with a jigsaw. When teaching a beginner, the jigsaw is the safer machine to use because of its slower cutting action. Moreover, jigsaw work is normally less than ¾ inch thick, leaving little room for a hand or finger to fit under the safety guard.

Disk Sander: The disk sander uses a flat, round sheet of sandpaper attached to a flat, platelike disk. Special disks may be mounted on drill presses, radial arm saws, or even on the wood lathe. Some disk sanders may have their own stand and motor and range in size from a 8-inch diameter disk for home use to the large 30-inch disk found in schools or industries. Disk sanders sand rapidly but tend to leave scratched rings on the wood surface.

Drum Sander: Drum sanders, also called spindle sanders, use a cylindrical drum to sand the edges of stock. With special attachments these drums may be attached to a drill press, radial arm saw, or a wood lathe for sanding. Larger drum sanders have their own motor, table, and base. Sanding drums for home use may be bought in ½- to 2-inch-diameter sizes.

Portable Belt Sander: The portable belt sander is a popular, lightweight, fast, and efficient means for sanding stock and, in some cases, assembled projects. A variety of belt grit textures is available in sizes ranging from 2 inches wide by 21 inches long to 4 inches wide by 27 inches long. Some belt sanders have a bag attached to collect the sawdust.

Helpful Hints

The toys in this book were designed to be simple in construction, moderately detailed, and attractive in appearance. They can be made in most home workshops.

Although many of the projects have numerous parts, only basic woodworking techniques are used. As these projects were being designed the following operations and tips came to mind that may help the novice woodworker.

MAKING WHEELS

The process of making wheels can be divided into three steps.

1. *Cut the wheel from the stock.* Mount a 2½-inch hole saw with a ¼-inch twist bit in the chuck of a drill press. Drill into a 2- by 4-inch piece of stock approximately 1¼ inches deep, or far enough so the twist bit on the hole saw drills through the bottom of the stock. Do not allow the hole saw to go completely through the stock or you will have difficulty getting the wheel out. Turn the board over and drill in from the bottom face, now turned up. Be sure the ¼-inch drill is aligned exactly over the ¼-inch hole. Drill into the stock until the wheel breaks off and protrudes enough to get a good grip on it for removal. Make as many wheels as needed for the particular toy under construction.

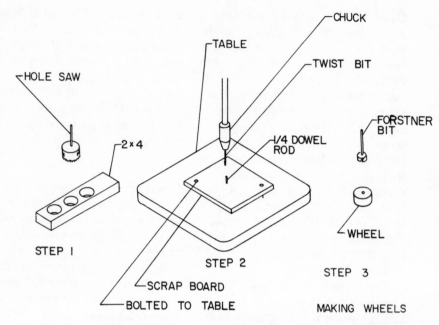

MAKING WHEELS

2. *Make a jig to center the wheel recesses.* Clamp a ¾-inch-thick scrap board on the table as shown. This board must be bolted or clamped to the table to prevent it from moving. Drill through the board using a ¼-inch twist bit. Remove the twist bit from the chuck. Place a ¼-inch dowel rod that is 1¼ inches long into the ¼-inch hole without moving the scrap board.

3. *Drill the portion of the wheel to be recessed.* Put a Forstner bit into the drill press. Its center should line up exactly with the center of the protruding ¼-inch dowel rod in the stationary scrap board. Raise the chuck and Forstner bit and place the wheel's ¼-inch hole into the ¼-inch dowel rod and press the wheel down onto the scrap board. Then drill into the wheel the specified depth using the Forst-

ner bit. This process will concentrically center the Forstner bit on the wheel's center.

PUSH STICK

Push sticks are safety devices commonly used with the table saw when ripping boards less than 4 inches wide. The notched end should be used to push the board while you hold the opposite end of the push stick; this will keep your hand at a safe distance from the blade. The thickness of push sticks may vary from ¼ to ¾ inch; they should always be less than the distance from the blade to the fence to prevent cutting the push stick. Paint the push sticks a bright color so they will not be thrown away as scrap wood.

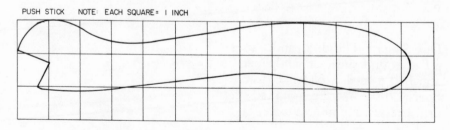

PUSH STICK   NOTE: EACH SQUARE = 1 INCH

CUTTING STOPS ON THE TABLE SAW

Stops can be made by clamping blocks of wood at a given point on a machine so that a board will start (stop A) and stop (stop B) at an identical point on each cut.

Shown in the accompanying illustration is the type of setup used in cutting the Cattle Car sides. Moving the fence to the right an equal distance on each cut, without moving the stops, will simplify cutting the grooves to equal lengths.

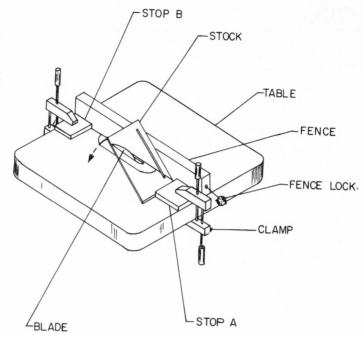

CUTTING STOPS ON THE
TABLE SAW

RESAWING

Resawing is a term used to describe the process of ripping a piece of stock to a thinner size. For example: take a board that is ¾ inch thick by 4 inches wide by 12 inches long. In making the trim pieces for the Coal Car on the train, this board could be planed to the required ³⁄₁₆-inch thickness leaving a board ³⁄₁₆ inch thick by 4 inches wide by 12 inches long from which to cut the trim. Planing the ¾-inch thick board to the ³⁄₁₆-inch thickness results in one board as the end product. Resawing or ripping the original ¾-inch thick board down the center, allowing ⅛ inch for the saw kerf (kerf means a saw cut), would produce two boards, each ⁵⁄₁₆ inch thick by 4 inches wide by 12 inches long. One of these could be planed to the correct dimensions. The second board, which would have become shavings if planed, is now also available for use in the project.

To resaw wood, make an L-shaped fence as shown in the accompanying illustration. Clamp or bolt it to the band saw table as shown and use it as a fence or guide while cutting the piece of stock to its new dimensions.

Many of the ¼-inch parts used in building the toys in this book were made from resawed lumber.

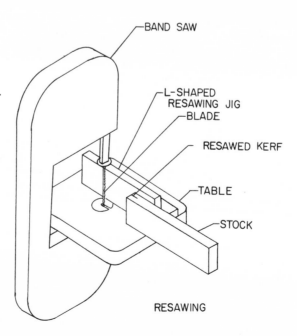

RESAWING

18

ENLARGING

Enlarging is the method used to increase the size of a pattern from a scale drawing to its actual size.

Throughout this book working drawings are laid out on graphs. The full-size dimension of each square accompanies each working drawing. To enlarge the pattern, simply draw the graph to its full size and sketch the pattern in as shown. Be sure that the lines intersect at approximately the same point on both graphs, regardless of the size of the block. This method helps you keep sizes and shapes proportionately correct.

CUTTING INSIDE CURVES

An inside curve can easily be cut using a jigsaw or coping saw, as shown. When using a jigsaw, drill a hole in the board to be cut. Then insert the jigsaw blade through the hole. While the blade is inside the board, fasten the jigsaw blade inside the upper chuck as well as into the lower chuck. If the board is large enough not to fall through the hole in the table, the throat plate need not be put back on the jigsaw until after the inside cut is completed.

When using a coping saw, drill the hole through the board. Take the blade out of the saw, place the blade through the hole, and reattach the blade in the saw. With the board secured in a vise or with clamps, cut out the design. Once completed, remove the blade from the saw, take it out of the stock, and put it back into the coping saw.

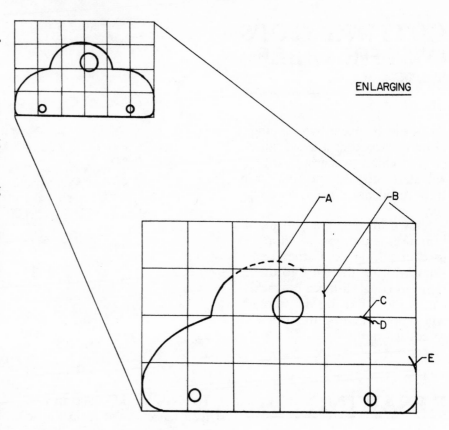

ENLARGING

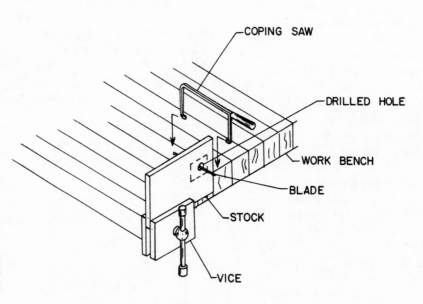

CUTTING INSIDE CURVES

CUTTING BEVELS

To cut the angles on the tops of the Train Cars, first cut the piece to size. If the pieces are smaller than 10 inches or the diameter of your table saw blade, cut a board longer than needed. This gives more bearing surface against the fence and thus is safer.

Once the stock has been cut to its overall size, cut two grooves into its face as shown. These should coordinate with the drawing and dimensions you are using.

Set the saw blade at the desired angle and cut from the edge of the stock to the first groove.

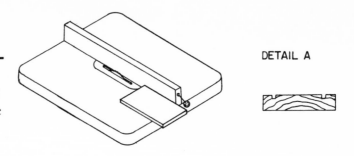

DETAIL A

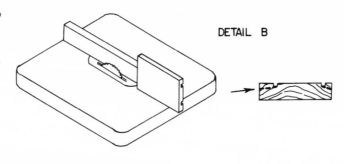

DETAIL B

CUTTING COVES

To cut a cove on a table saw, clamp a scrap board to act as a fence to the table as shown. This board must have a perfectly straight edge on the side being used as a fence. The angle at which it is clamped will determine the curved shape of the cove. Practice cutting coves on scrap wood first to be sure the angle at which the fence is set produces the shape you want. Adjust the angle of the fence until you achieve the right curve.

After the fence is clamped at the appropriate angle, raise the blade so it protrudes above the table $\frac{1}{16}$ to $\frac{1}{8}$ inch. Slide your stock from right to left over the blade, using the fence as a guide. This will produce a small, curved cut on the bottom of the stock.

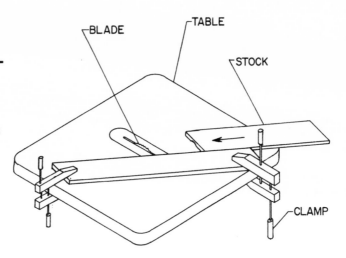

CUTTING A COVE ON THE TABLE SAW

Repeat this process, raising the blade slightly on each cut, until the desired depth is reached. As you push the board across the blade, hold the board on its end with the notched end of a push stick. If the stick is in the wrong spot or you slip, the push stick will be cut, not your hand.

PART TWO

TOY PROJECTS

Steam Engine

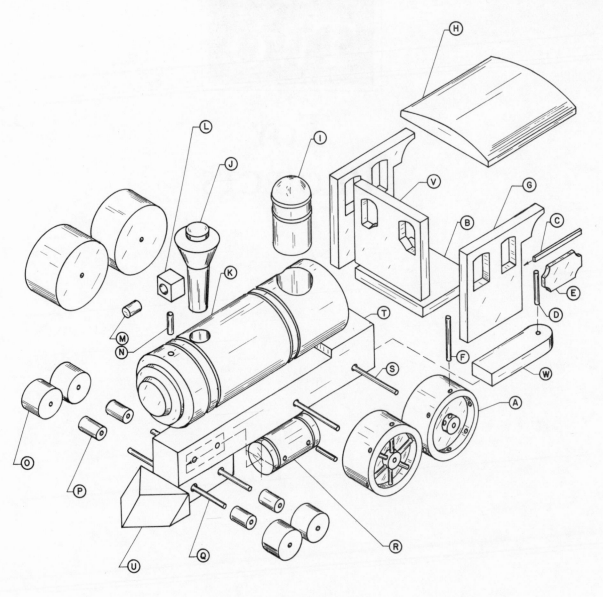

Above: Autos (see page 46)

Left: Motorcycle (see page 60)

Below left: Jeep (see page 83)

A

Right: Box Car (see page 34)

Middle right: Cattle Car (see page 38)

Far right: Flat-Bed Car (see page 47)

Far left: Steam Engine (see page 22)

Middle left: Tender (see page 28)

Left: Coal Car (see page 31)

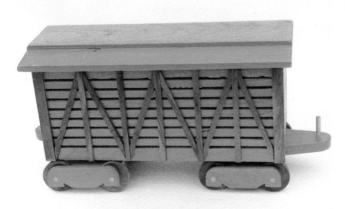

Far left: Gondola Car (see page 50)

Left: Tanker Car (see page 53)

Right: Caboose (see page 56)

C

Above, top: Semi-Tractor (see page 88) and Flat-Bed Trailer (see page 92)

Above: Semi-Tractor and Enclosed Trailer (see page 94)

Left: Tractor (see page 103)

MATERIALS

LETTER	NUMBER REQUIRED	NAME	SIZE
A	4	BACK WHEEL	3⅛ × 3⅛ × 1⅞ inches
B	1	CAB BASE	4¹¹⁄₁₆ × 3⅞ × ½ inches
C	2	WINDOW SILL	2¾ × ³⁄₁₆ × ¼ inches
D	1	HITCH	¼-inch dowel, 2 inches long
E	2	SIDE TRIM	1½ × 2¾ × ³⁄₁₆ inches
F	12	SPOKES	¼-inch dowel, 1½ inches long
G	2	CAB SIDE	5⅜ × 5¼ × ½ inches
H	1	CAB TOP	6¼ × 6 × ¾ inches
I	1	STEAM DOME	3½ × 2¹⁄₁₆ × 2¹⁄₁₆ inches
J	1	SMOKESTACK	4⅞ × 2¾ × 2¾ inches
K	1	BOILER	11¼ × 3¾ × 3¾ inches
L	1	LIGHT BOX	¾ × ¾ × ¾ inches
M	1	LIGHT	½-inch dowel, ½ inch long
N	1	LIGHT POST	¼-inch dowel, ¾ inch long
O	4	FRONT WHEEL	1¾ × 1¾ × ¾ inches
P	4	SPACER	¾-inch dowel, 1 inch long
Q	2	FRONT AXLE	¼-inch dowel, 5¼ inches long
R	2	PISTON	3½ × 1⅝ × 1⅝ inches
S	2	BACK AXLE	¼-inch dowel, 5¾ inches long
T	1	BASE	14 × 2⅜ × 1⅞ inches
U	2	CATTLE CATCHER	7½ × 3½ × 1½ inches
V	1	CAB FRONT	4¹¹⁄₁₆ × 4¾ × ½ inches
W	1	HITCH STEM	5 × 1½ × ½ inches

Two No. 10 finishing nails
Two No. 4 finishing nails
Thirty 1-inch wire brads
Twenty ½-inch wire brads
Two 3½-inch hex-headed lag
   bolts

TOOLS

Hammer
Nail set
Coping saw
Block plane
Try square
Ruler
Compass
Lathe
Table saw
Electric drill
2-inch hole saw
$\frac{3}{8}$-inch twist bit
$\frac{1}{4}$-inch twist bit
$\frac{1}{2}$-inch twist bit
2-inch spade bit
1-inch spade bit

CONSTRUCTION NOTES

Base
Parts D, T, U, and W

Cut out part T, the base, using a table saw. Drill the holes for the back axles using an electric drill and twist bit. Part U, the cattle catcher, can also be made with the table saw. Cut the angles first while the piece of stock is longer than necessary, to ensure a safer cutting operation. Cut the notch in part U using the table saw. Drill the hole in part U for the front axles using a twist bit and an electric drill. Attach part U to part T, the base, at the bottom with glue and two No. 10 finishing nails. The cattle catcher should fit 4 inches back from the front of part T.

The hitch stem, part W, can be cut out using the table saw and a coping saw. Drill the hole with a twist bit and an electric drill. Part W should be centered from side to side and glued and nailed to the bottom of part T, leaving 3 inches of the rounded end of part W protruding from the back of part T.

Use a coping saw to cut part D. Glue part D into part W so part D is flush on the bottom of part W.

PART D

PART T

PART U

PART W

Piston
Part R

Turn the piston, part R, on a wood lathe. Attach it with two dowel rods 2⅝ inches long. The piston is located ½ inch from the front edge of part T, the base. It should be centered vertically on part T. Drill the first hole through part R and into part T in one operation. Put a dowel rod in one hole. Then drill the second hole through both R and T and insert the second dowel. This method will ensure alignment of the holes on the piston and base.

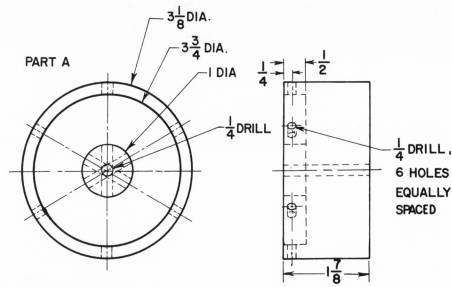

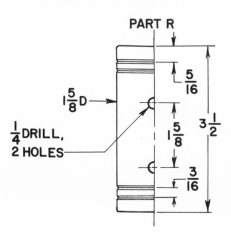

Front Wheel
Parts O, P, and Q

The front wheels, part O, are cut using a hole saw and an electric drill. Next cut a dowel rod for part P, the spacers, with a coping saw. Drill the center hole through part P using a twist bit and an electric drill. Cut part Q, the front axles, to length with a coping saw. Slide part Q through part U, the cattle catcher. Place a spacer on each side of part Q, flush to part U. Then glue a wheel on each end of the dowel rod so the dowel rod and wheel are flush on the outside. The axle should turn in the hole of the cattle catcher.

Back Wheel
Parts A, F, and S

Turn part A, the back wheels, on a face plate of a lathe. Drill the holes for part F, the spokes, into part A using a twist bit and an electric drill. Cut a dowel rod for part S, the back axles and part F, the spokes, using a coping saw. Very carefully glue the spokes, part F, into the holes in the back wheels, part A. Tap these in lightly, being careful not to break the wheels. After all the spokes are assembled, insert the axles into the axle holes on part T. Glue the wheels on the back axles, part S, leaving part A flush on the end of the axle.

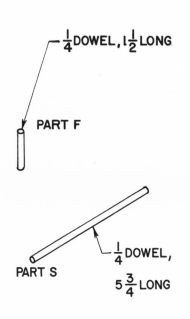

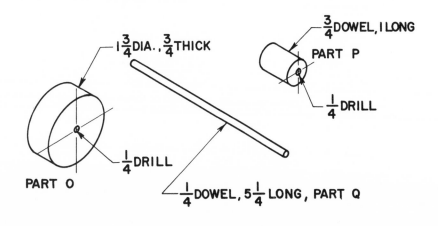

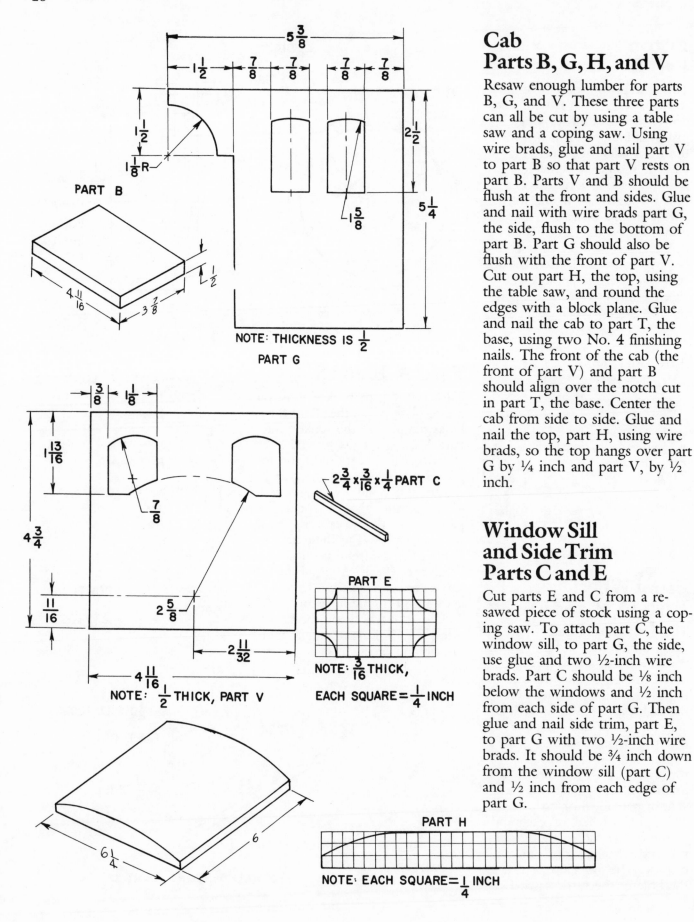

PART B

$4\frac{11}{16}$ $3\frac{7}{8}$ $\frac{1}{2}$

$5\frac{3}{8}$ $1\frac{1}{2}$ $\frac{7}{8}$ $\frac{7}{8}$ $\frac{7}{8}$ $\frac{7}{8}$

$1\frac{1}{2}$ $1\frac{1}{8}$R $2\frac{1}{2}$ $5\frac{1}{4}$ $1\frac{5}{8}$

NOTE: THICKNESS IS $\frac{1}{2}$
PART G

$\frac{3}{8}$ $1\frac{1}{8}$ $1\frac{13}{16}$ $4\frac{3}{4}$ $\frac{7}{8}$ $\frac{11}{16}$ $2\frac{5}{8}$ $2\frac{11}{32}$ $4\frac{11}{16}$

NOTE: $\frac{1}{2}$ THICK, PART V

$2\frac{3}{4} \times \frac{3}{16} \times \frac{1}{4}$ PART C

PART E

NOTE: $\frac{3}{16}$ THICK,
EACH SQUARE = $\frac{1}{4}$ INCH

$6\frac{1}{4}$ 6

PART H

NOTE: EACH SQUARE = $\frac{1}{4}$ INCH

Cab
Parts B, G, H, and V

Resaw enough lumber for parts B, G, and V. These three parts can all be cut by using a table saw and a coping saw. Using wire brads, glue and nail part V to part B so that part V rests on part B. Parts V and B should be flush at the front and sides. Glue and nail with wire brads part G, the side, flush to the bottom of part B. Part G should also be flush with the front of part V. Cut out part H, the top, using the table saw, and round the edges with a block plane. Glue and nail the cab to part T, the base, using two No. 4 finishing nails. The front of the cab (the front of part V) and part B should align over the notch cut in part T, the base. Center the cab from side to side. Glue and nail the top, part H, using wire brads, so the top hangs over part G by ¼ inch and part V, by ½ inch.

Window Sill
and Side Trim
Parts C and E

Cut parts E and C from a resawed piece of stock using a coping saw. To attach part C, the window sill, to part G, the side, use glue and two ½-inch wire brads. Part C should be ⅛ inch below the windows and ½ inch from each side of part G. Then glue and nail side trim, part E, to part G with two ½-inch wire brads. It should be ¾ inch down from the window sill (part C) and ½ inch from each edge of part G.

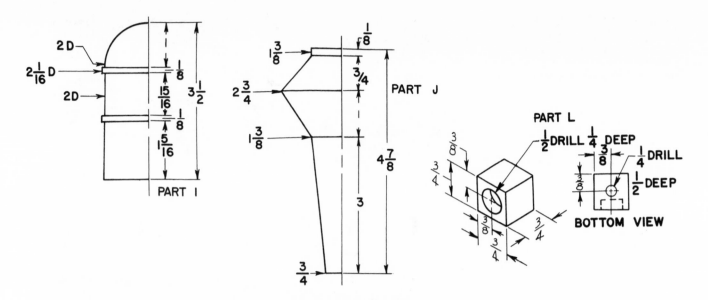

Boiler
Parts I, J, K, L, M, N

The boiler, part K, should be turned on a lathe. Drill the hole for the steam dome, part I, and the hole for the smokestack, part J, using either a spade bit or a Forstner bit. Drill the hole for part N, the light post, using a twist bit. Attach the boiler with two 3½-inch-long hex-headed lag bolts screwed in from the bottom of part T, the base. It

should fit snugly against part V, the front cab. Predrill holes for the lag bolts to prevent breaking part T or part K.

Part I, the steam dome, should be turned on a lathe. Glue and fit it snugly into the hole on the boiler, part K. Allow it to protrude from the boiler approximately 2½ inches.

Turn part J, the smokestack, on the lathe also. It should be glued into part K, protruding approximately 3⅞ inches.

Cut part L, the light box, using the table saw. Drill the holes for the light, part M, and the light post, part N, into part L using a twist bit and an electric drill. Cut the light and the light post from dowel rods using a coping saw. Glue part M into part L leaving ⅛ inch protruding. Glue part N into the boiler, part K, and into the light box, part L, leaving ⅛ inch between the boiler and the light box.

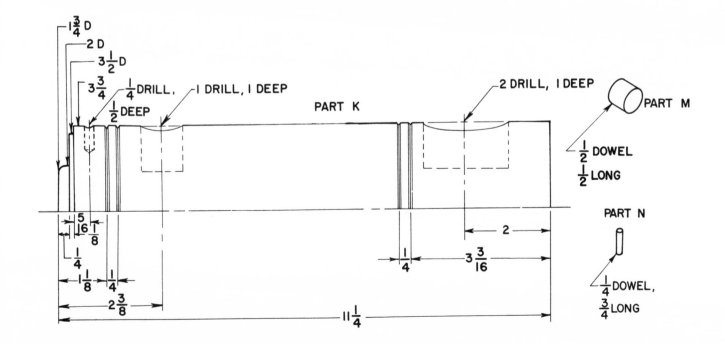

Tender

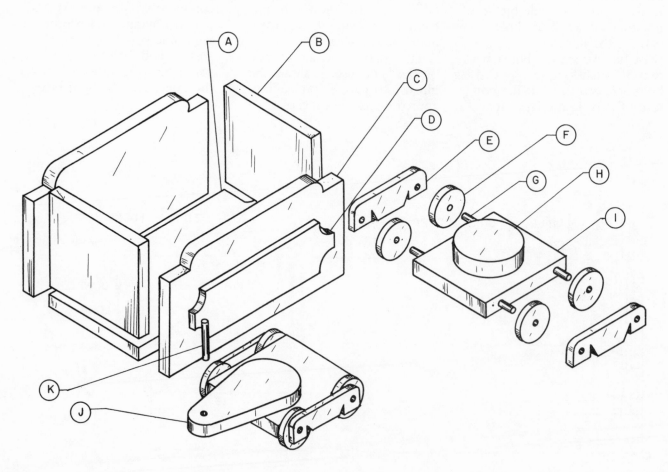

MATERIALS

LETTER	NUMBER REQUIRED	NAME	SIZE
A	1	BOTTOM	10⅜ × 4⅝ × ½ inches
B	2	END	4 × 4⅝ × ½ inches
C	2	SIDE	8⅞ × 5⅛ × ½ inches
D	2	RAISED PANEL	7 × 2½ × ¼ inches
E	4	WHEEL COVER	3⅝ × 1 × ¼ inches
F	8	WHEEL	1½ × 1½ × ¼ inches
G	8	AXLE	¼-inch dowel, 1½ inches long
H	1	BACK SPACER	2½ × 2½ × ½ inch thick
I	2	AXLE HOUSING	4 × 3⅝ × ¾ inches
J	1	FRONT SPACER	5 × 2½ × ½ inches
K	1	HITCH	¼-inch dowel, 1½ inches long

Thirty 1-inch wire brads
Four ½-inch wire brads

TOOLS

Ruler
Try square
C-clamps
Nail set
Hammer
Electric drill

Table saw
Coping saw
2½-inch hole saw
1¾-inch hole saw
¼-inch twist bit

CONSTRUCTION NOTES

Bottom, End, and Side Parts A, B, and C

Cut parts A, B, and C with a table saw. Use a coping saw to cut the curves on part C. Using wire brads, glue and nail the ends, part B, to the bottom, part A, flush to the ends of part A. Glue and nail the sides, part C, so they cover the edge of part B, the end, and part A, the bottom. The bottom edge of part C should be flush with the bottom of part A.

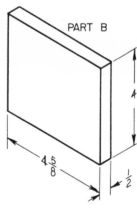

PART B

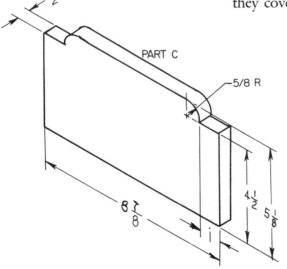

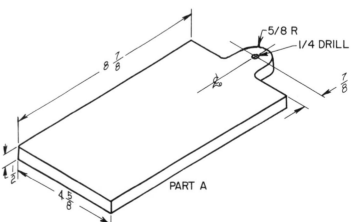

Axle Housing
Parts H, I, J, and K

Cut the axle housing, part I, on a table saw. Drill the holes for the axle using a twist bit and an electric drill. Cut the back spacer, part H, using a hole saw. Glue and clamp the back spacer to part I so it is approximately ¾ inch from each edge of part I.

Cut the front spacer, part J, using a coping saw. Drill the hole for part K, the hitch, using an electric drill and twist bit. Attach part J, the front spacer, to part I, the axle housing, so part J is ¾ inch from each side of part I and 1 inch from the back of part I. Cut a dowel rod for part K, the hitch, and glue part K into the hole in part J, flush with the bottom of part J. Glue and clamp (C-clamps) part J, the front spacer, and part H, the back spacer, to the bottom, part A. The ends of part I, the axle housing, should be even with the ends of part C, the sides. Part I, the axle housing, should also be centered from side to side on the bottom, part A.

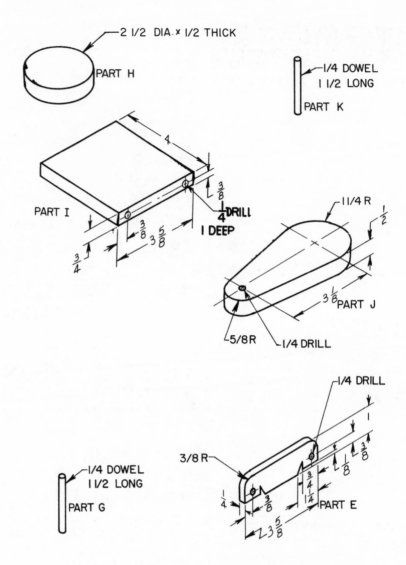

Raised Panel
Part D

Using a table saw, resaw the piece of stock used for part D to its correct thickness. Cut the raised panel with a coping saw. Using ½-inch wire brads, glue and nail the raised panel to the side, part C, 1 inch from each end of part C and 1⅛ inches from the top of part C.

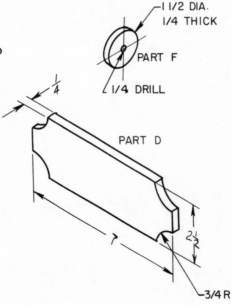

Wheel and Axle
Parts E, F, and G

Resaw the stock for part F, the wheels, using a table saw. Cut the wheels using a hole saw and an electric drill. Cut the axles, part G, with a coping saw. Glue the axles, part G, into the axle housing, part I, so part G protrudes from the axle housing by 9/16 inch. Part F, the wheels, rotates around part G, which is stationary. Slide the wheels, part F, over the axle, part G, then glue part E on the end of the axle, part G. Part E should be flush on the outside with the end of the axle, part G.

Coal Car

MATERIALS

LETTER	NUMBER REQUIRED	NAME	SIZE
A	1	HITCH	¼-inch dowel, 1½ inches long
B	1	FRONT SPACER	5⅛ × 2½ × ½ inches
C	2	AXLE HOUSING	4 × 3⅝ × ¾ inches
D	8	WHEEL	1½ × 1½ × ¼ inches
E	4	WHEEL COVER	3⅝ × 1 × ¼ inches
F	1	FRONT BED	4⅝ × 3⁹⁄₁₆ × ½ inches
G	8	AXLE	¼-inch dowel, 1½ inches long
H	1	BACK SPACER	2½ × 2½ × ½ inches
I	10	VERTICAL TRIM	3¾ × ¼ × ³⁄₁₆ inches
J	4	HORIZONTAL TRIM	12 × ¼ × ³⁄₁₆ inches
K	2	END	4⅝ × ⅜ × 1¼ inches
L	2	SIDE	12 × 4¼ × ⅜ inches
M	2	DIAGONAL	6 × 4⅝ × ½ inches
N	2	BOTTOM DETAIL	3½ × ¾ × ¼ inches
O	1	BACK BED	4⅝ × 5¹⁄₁₆ × ½ inches

Thirty ½-inch wire brads
Forty 1-inch wire brads

TOOLS

Coping saw
Try square
Ruler
Compass
Hammer
Nail set

Table saw
Jointer
Electric drill or drill press
2½-inch hole saw
1¾-inch hole saw
¼-inch twist bit

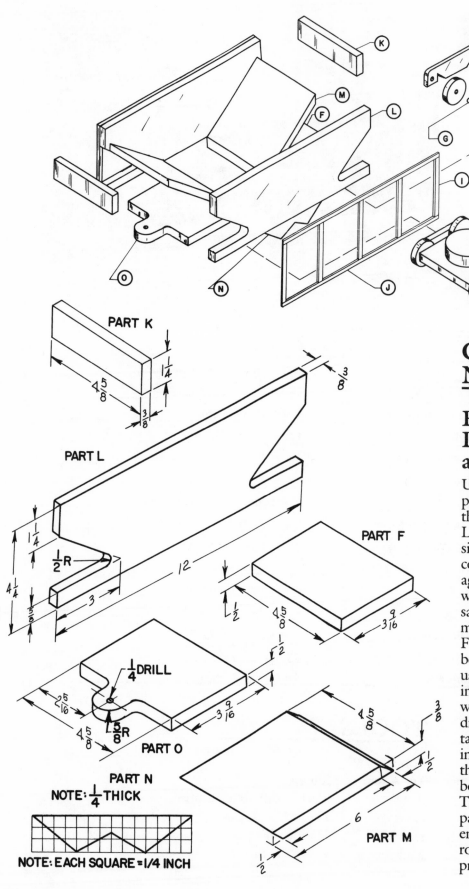

PART K

PART L

PART F

$\frac{1}{2}$R

12

3

PART O

$\frac{1}{4}$ DRILL

$\frac{5}{8}$R

PART N

NOTE: $\frac{1}{4}$ THICK

NOTE: EACH SQUARE = 1/4 INCH

PART M

6

CONSTRUCTION NOTES

Bed and Sides Parts F, K, L, M, N, and O

Using a jointer or table saw, plane or resaw enough stock to the required thicknesses for parts L, M, and K. Cut part L, the sides, with a table saw and a coping saw. Cut part M, the di-agonals, and part K, the ends, with a table saw. Plane and re-saw enough stock to the recom-mended thickness to make parts F and O. Cut part F, the front bed, and part O, the back bed, using the table saw and the cop-ing saw. Drill the hole in part O with a twist bit and an electric drill. Cut part N, the bottom de-tail, using a table saw and a cop-ing saw. Glue and nail part L, the side, to part O, the back bed, with their bottoms flush. The square outside portion of part O should be flush with the ends of part L, leaving the rounded hitch portion of part O protruding as shown.

Glue and nail part F, the front bed, to part L, the side, keeping the bottoms and ends flush. Glue and nail part K, the ends, onto part L, the sides, making part K flush with the top and end of part L. Glue and nail the diagonals, part M, onto part L, the sides. Part M should fit tightly against part K, at an angle parallel to but ⅛ inch above the angle on part L. The diagonals should be 1¼ inches apart at their base. Part M should now protrude from the bottom of part L by approximately ⅜ to ½ inch. Glue and nail part N to the diagonals, part M, so part N touches part L, the sides, and is approximately centered on part L from end to end.

Trim
Parts I and J

Using a table saw, cut part I, the vertical trim, and part J, the horizontal trim. With ½-inch wire brads, carefully nail one piece o part J to the top of part L, so part J is flush on the top and both ends of part L, the sides. Nail the second piece of part J to the side of part L at the bottom, leaving it flush on the bottom and both ends of part L. Glue and nail part I, the vertical trim, to each side of part L and at intervals of 3 inches as shown.

Axle Housing
Parts A, B, C, and H

Cut the axle housing, part C, using a table saw. Drill the holes ⅞ inch deep with an electric drill and a twist bit. Cut part H, the back spacer, with a hole saw and an electric drill or drill press. Cut part B, the front spacer, with a coping saw; drill the hole with a twist bit and an electric drill. Cut part A, the hitch, from a dowel rod using a coping saw. Glue part A, the hitch, into part B, the front spacer, with bottoms flush. Nail part B, the front spacer, to part C, the first axle housing, using 1-inch wire brads. Part B should extend from part C by 2 inches and be centered on part C from side to side.

Glue and nail part H, the back spacer, to the center of part C, the second axle housing, as shown in the illustration. Glue part H, the back spacer, to part O, the back bed, so part C, the back axle housing, is aligned with the straight portion of part O, the back bed. Glue the top of part B, the front spacer, to the bottom of part F, the front bed, so part C and part F are flush, with part C centered from side to side.

Wheel and Axle
Parts D, E, and G

Cut the wheels, part D, using a 1¾-inch hole saw and an electric drill. Cut part G, the axle, from a dowel rod using a coping saw. Cut part E, the wheel cover, to its correct thickness with a table saw; then use a coping saw to round the corners and cut the shape; drill the holes using an electric drill and a twist bit. Glue part G, the axle, into the axle housing, part C, leaving part G protruding ⅝ inch. Slide the wheel, part D, onto the axle, part G. Glue part E on the axle, keeping the ends of part G flush with the outside surface of part E.

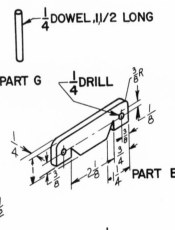

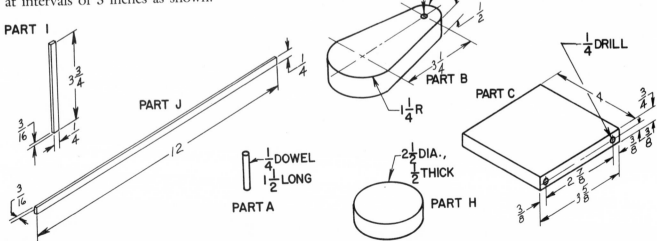

Box Car

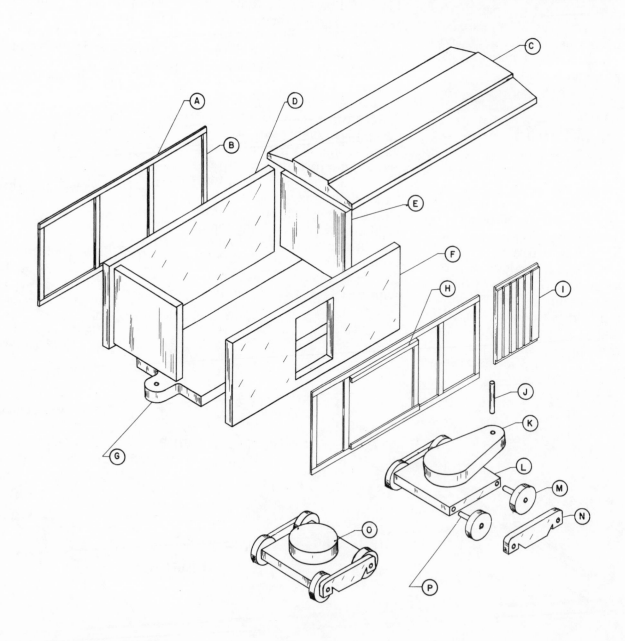

MATERIALS

LETTER	NUMBER REQUIRED	NAME	SIZE
A	4	HORIZONTAL TRIM	12 × ¼ × ³⁄₁₆ inches
B	9	VERTICAL TRIM	4½ × ¼ × ³⁄₁₆ inches
C	1	TOP	13 × 6 × ¾ inches
D	1	SIDE	12 × 5 × ½ inches
E	2	END	4½ × 4⅝ × ½ inches
F	1	SIDE WITH DOOR	12 × 5 × ½ inches
G	1	BOTTOM	13½ × 4⅝ × ½ inches
H	4	DOOR TRACK	6 × ⅜ × ⅜ inches
I	1	DOOR	3¾ × 3 × ¼ inches
J	1	HITCH	¼-inch dowel, 1½ inches long
K	1	FRONT SPACER	5 × 2½ × ½ inches
L	2	AXLE HOUSING	3⅝ × 4 × ¾ inches
M	8	WHEEL	1½ × 1½ × ¼ inches
N	4	WHEEL COVER	3⅝ × 1 × ¼ inches
O	1	BACK SPACER	2½ × 2½ × ½ inches
P	8	AXLE	¼-inch dowel, 1½ inches long

Thirty 1-inch wire brads
Thirty ½-inch wire brads

TOOLS

Hammer
Nail set
Ruler
Compass
Try square
Coping saw
Table saw
Electric drill
¼-inch twist bit
2½-inch hole saw
1¾-inch hole saw

CONSTRUCTION NOTES

Box
Parts C, D, E, F, and G

Resaw a piece of stock large enough to make parts E, F, G, and D to a ½-inch thickness. Cut the bottom, part G, on a table saw; use a coping saw to cut the curves. Drill the hole using an electric drill and a twist bit. Cut part E, the ends, part F, the side with the door, and part D, the side, with a table saw. Drill a starting hole in the door section of part F and then use a coping saw to cut out the center portion, the hole for the door. Part C, the top, may be cut using a table saw; see the chapter titled Helpful Hints on cutting bevels.

Glue and nail the ends, part E, onto the bottom, part G, flush with the rectangular part of part G. Glue and nail the sides, parts F and D, onto the edge of part E, the ends, and part G, the bottom. The sides should be flush with the ends and at the bottom of part G. You should now have a box with two sides and two ends that are flush on top. Place part C, the top, on the top of the box, leaving a ¼-inch overhang on the sides and a ½-inch overhang on each end. Glue and nail part C, the top, to the sides and ends with 1-inch wire brads.

36

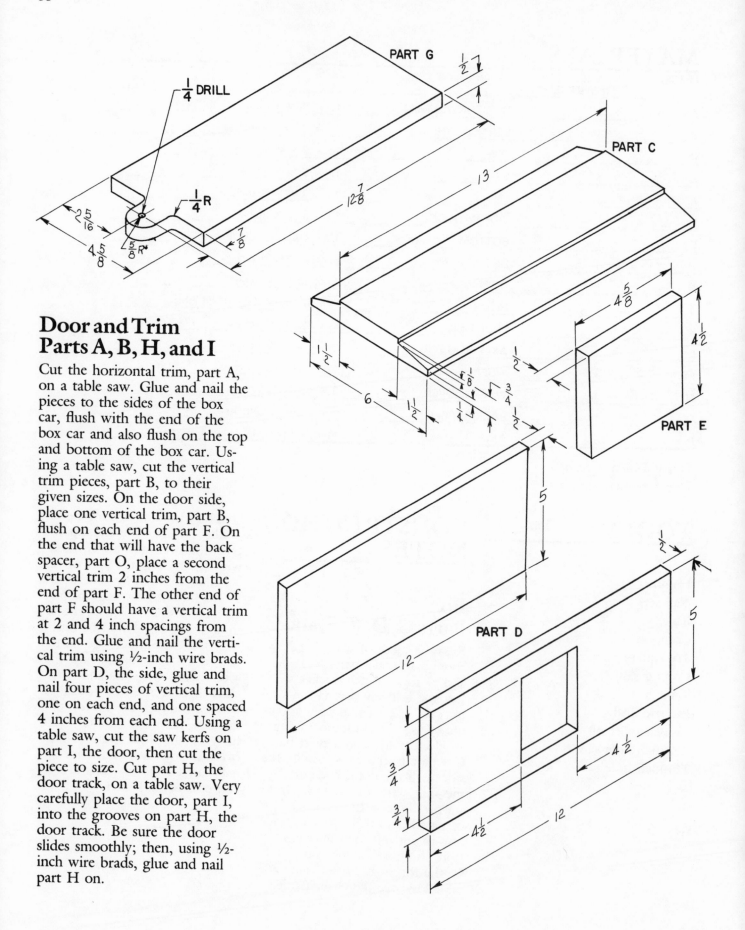

PART G

¼ DRILL

$2\frac{5}{16}$

$4\frac{5}{8}$

$\frac{5}{8}$ R

¼ R

$\frac{7}{8}$

$12\frac{7}{8}$

13

PART C

$\frac{1}{2}$

$1\frac{1}{2}$

6

$1\frac{1}{2}$

$\frac{1}{8}$

$\frac{1}{4}$

$\frac{3}{4}$

$\frac{1}{2}$

$\frac{1}{2}$

$4\frac{5}{8}$

$4\frac{1}{2}$

PART E

5

Door and Trim
Parts A, B, H, and I

Cut the horizontal trim, part A, on a table saw. Glue and nail the pieces to the sides of the box car, flush with the end of the box car and also flush on the top and bottom of the box car. Using a table saw, cut the vertical trim pieces, part B, to their given sizes. On the door side, place one vertical trim, part B, flush on each end of part F. On the end that will have the back spacer, part O, place a second vertical trim 2 inches from the end of part F. The other end of part F should have a vertical trim at 2 and 4 inch spacings from the end. Glue and nail the vertical trim using ½-inch wire brads. On part D, the side, glue and nail four pieces of vertical trim, one on each end, and one spaced 4 inches from each end. Using a table saw, cut the saw kerfs on part I, the door, then cut the piece to size. Cut part H, the door track, on a table saw. Very carefully place the door, part I, into the grooves on part H, the door track. Be sure the door slides smoothly; then, using ½-inch wire brads, glue and nail part H on.

PART D

12

$\frac{1}{2}$

5

$\frac{3}{4}$

$\frac{3}{4}$

$4\frac{1}{2}$

$4\frac{1}{2}$

12

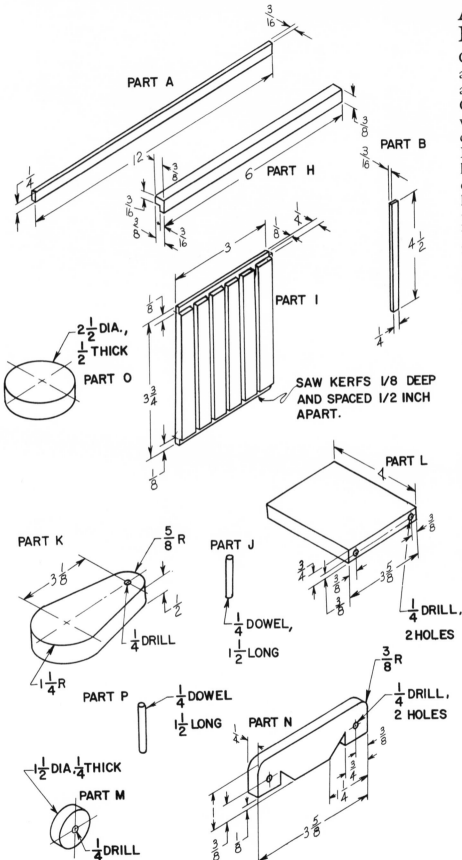

PART A

3/16

PART H

12

6

1/4

3/8

3/8

3/16

PART B

3/16

4 1/2

1/4

3

1/8

1/4

PART I

1/8

3 3/4

1/8

SAW KERFS 1/8 DEEP
AND SPACED 1/2 INCH
APART.

2 1/2 DIA.,
1/2 THICK

PART O

PART L

4

3/4 1/4

3/8
3/8

3 5/8

3/8

1/4 DRILL,
2 HOLES

PART K

5/8 R

3 1/8

1/2

1/4 DRILL

1 1/4 R

PART J

1/4 DOWEL,
1 1/2 LONG

PART P

1/4 DOWEL
1 1/2 LONG

PART N

1/4

3/8 R

1/4 DRILL,
2 HOLES

3/8

3/4

1/4

3/8 1/8

3 5/8

1 1/2 DIA. 1/4 THICK

PART M

1/4 DRILL

Axle Housing
Parts J, K, L, and O

Cut the axle housing, part L, on a table saw; drill the holes using a twist bit and an electric drill. Cut part O, the back spacer, with a hole saw and an electric drill. Cut the front spacer, part K, with a coping saw; drill the hole using a twist bit and an electric drill. Cut part J, the hitch, with a coping saw; glue part J into the hole on part K, the front spacer, with bottoms flush. Center and glue part O, the back spacer, to part L, the axle housing. Glue part K to part L, allowing 2 inches of part K to protrude from part L; part K should be centered from side to side on part L.

Wheel
Parts M, N, and P

Cut the wheel, part M, using a hole saw and an electric drill. Cut the axle, part P, with a coping saw. Cut part N to its correct thickness on the table saw; then use a coping saw to round the corners and cut the shape. Drill the two holes in part N with an electric drill and a twist bit. Glue the axles into part L, the axle housing, so they protrude from the holes by 5/8 inch. Slide the wheels onto the axle, part P; do not let any glue get on the wheels. Glue would prevent the wheels from turning. Glue part N, the wheel cover, onto the axle, part P, with the ends of the axle flush on the outside of part N. Glue and clamp part O, the back spacer, and part K, the front spacer, onto the bottom, part G. Part L, the axle housing, should align on each end with the ends of the box car, centered from side to side.

Cattle Car

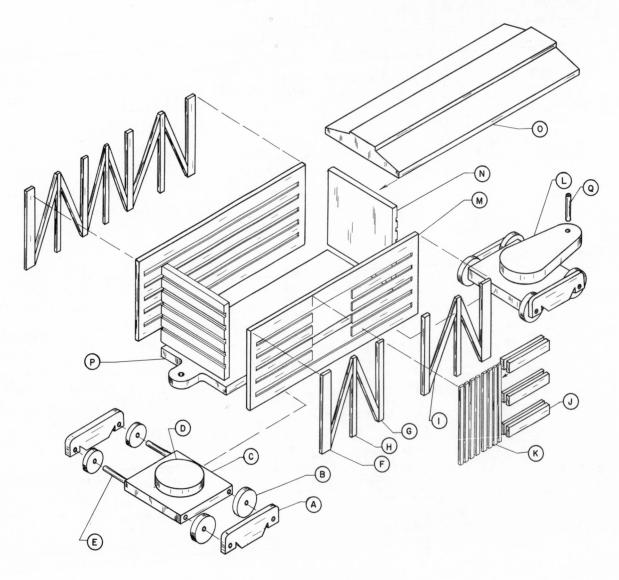

MATERIALS

LETTER	NUMBER REQUIRED	NAME	SIZE
A	4	WHEEL COVER	3⅝ × 1 × ¼ inches
B	8	WHEEL	1½ × 1½ × ¼ inches
C	2	AXLE HOUSING	3⅝ × 4 × ¾ inches
D	1	BACK SPACER	2½ × 2½ × ½ inches
E	8	AXLE	¼-inch dowel, 2 inches long
F	4	TRIM	4⅞ × 7⁄16 × ¼ inches
G	4	TRIM	4⅞ × ⅜ × ¼ inches
H	4	TRIM	4⅞ × 3⁄16 × ¼ inches
I	10	TRIM	5¼ × 3⁄16 × ¼ inches
J	6	HORIZONTAL DOOR TRIM	2⅞ × ⅜ × ¼ inches
K	8	DOOR UPRIGHT	3⁹⁄16 × ⅛ × 3⁄32 inches
L	1	FRONT SPACER	5 × 2½ × ½ inches
M	2	SIDE	11⅞ × 4⅞ × ¼ inches
N	2	END	4⅝ × 4⅞ × ½ inches
O	1	TOP	12¾ × 6 × ¾ inches
P	1	BOTTOM	13⅜ × 4⅝ × ½ inches
Q	1	HITCH	¼-inch dowel, 1½ inches long

Forty 1-inch wire brads

TOOLS

Ruler
Try square
Hammer
Compass
Coping saw
C-clamps or hand screw clamps
Electric drill
Table saw
¼-inch twist bit
2½-inch hole saw
1¾-inch hole saw

CONSTRUCTION NOTES

Bottom, Side, End, and Top Parts M, N, O, and P

Resaw enough lumber on a table saw to a ½-inch thickness to make parts P and N. Cut out part P, the bottom, using a table saw and a coping saw. Drill the hole for part Q, the hitch, with an electric drill and a twist bit. Cut the ends, part N, to size on a table saw. The saw kerfs can easily be cut on the table saw; use a push stick for safety since the pieces are small. Using wire brads, glue and nail the end, part N, onto the end of part P, the bottom. The ends of parts P and N should be flush except for the protruding hitch section of part P.

Resaw enough stock to make part M, the side, using a table saw. Cut the saw kerfs, making sure that they go through the stock. See the cutting stops section of the chapter titled Helpful Hints for more detailed instructions. Lay out the door opening on one side but do not cut it until the trim is in place. Do not glue or nail the sides on at this time. Cut the top, part O, on the table saw. Again consult the Helpful Hints chapter for information about cutting bevels.

40

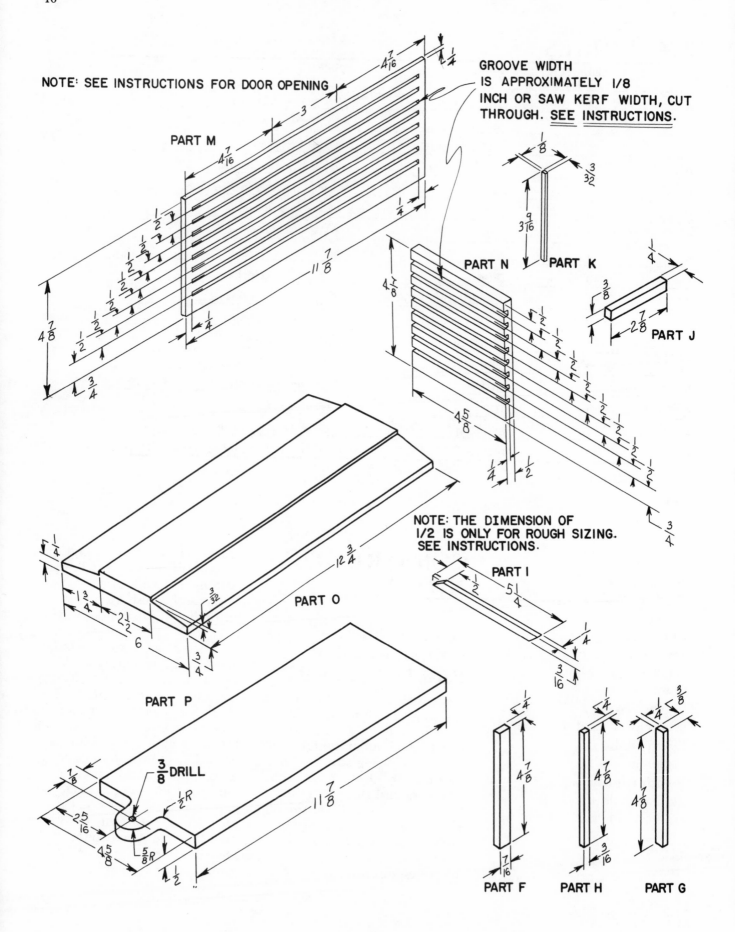

NOTE: SEE INSTRUCTIONS FOR DOOR OPENING

GROOVE WIDTH IS APPROXIMATELY 1/8 INCH OR SAW KERF WIDTH, CUT THROUGH. SEE INSTRUCTIONS.

PART M

PART N   PART K

PART J

NOTE: THE DIMENSION OF 1/2 IS ONLY FOR ROUGH SIZING. SEE INSTRUCTIONS.

PART I

PART O

PART P

3/8 DRILL

PART F   PART H   PART G

Trim
Parts F, G, H, and I

Cut parts F, G, H, and I into long resawed strips on the table saw, making each the correct width and depth. Then carefully cut part F, the trim, using the table saw. Glue and clamp part F to the side, part M, so the ends are flush. Glue and clamp part G, the trim, in the same manner. After the glue has dried, cut the door opening on one side using a coping saw. Cut part H, the trim, on a table saw and glue part H to part M, centered between parts G and F. Then cut the angles for part I, the trim, with the table saw. Glue and clamp part I to part M.

Door
Parts J and K

Cut the pieces for part K, the door uprights, and part J, the horizontal door trim, on the table saw. Glue the pieces of the door, using hand screw clamps or C-clamps. Attach the door to the side, part M, inside the door opening by driving a wire brad through part M and into part J, the horizontal door trim. This should be done on top and bottom of the door opening so the brads hit the door on the inside of part J about ⅛ inch from the end of part J. This will allow the door to pivot.

   Once the door pivots satisfactorily, glue and nail with wire brads part M, the side, to part P, the bottom, and part N, the ends. The bottom surfaces of parts M and P should be flush. The bottom and end surfaces of part M and part N should be flush. Glue and nail part O, the top, onto part N, the ends, and part M, the sides. Part O should hang over part N about ⅜ inch

and hang over part M about ⅛ inch.

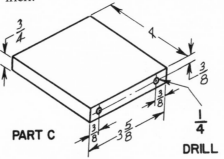

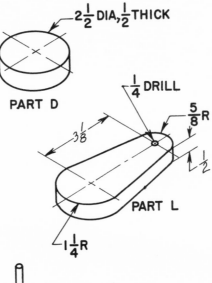

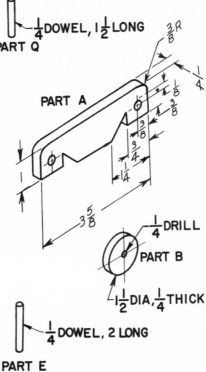

Axle Housing
Parts C, D, L, and Q

Cut the axle housing, part C, using a table saw. Drill the holes with an electric drill and a twist bit. Cut part D, the back spacer, from a piece of resawed ½-inch stock using an electric drill and a 2½-inch hole saw. Glue and nail part D to part C, centering part D on part C. Cut out part L, the front spacer, from a piece of resawed ½-inch stock with a coping saw. Drill the hole in part L with a twist bit and an electric drill. Glue and nail part L to part C so part L is centered on part C from side to side and extends past part C 2 inches. Cut part Q, the hitch, using a coping saw. Glue part Q into the hole in part L, the front spacer, with bottoms flush.

Wheel
Parts A, B, and E

Cut the wheels, part B, from a piece of ¼-inch stock using a 1¾-inch hole saw and an electric drill. Cut part E, the axles, to the proper length with a coping saw. Resaw enough stock to cut part A. Cut part A with a coping saw, using an electric drill and twist bit to drill the holes required. Glue the axles, part E, into the axle housing, part C, so the axles extend ⅝ inch. Slide the wheel, part B, over the axle, making sure no glue gets on the wheel. Then glue part A onto part E so that the outside surfaces of parts A and E are flush. Glue and clamp part D, the back spacer, and part L, the front spacer, to the bottom, part P, so part C, the axle housing, is flush with each end of part P.

Auto Carrier Car

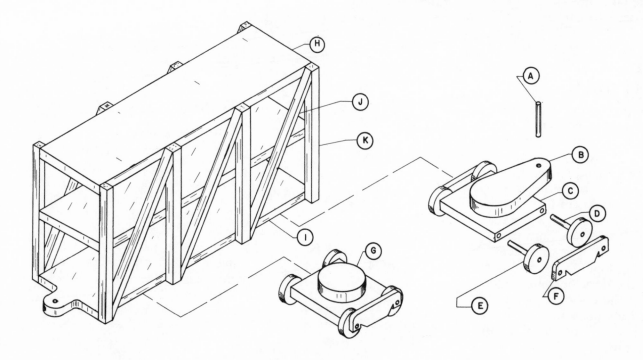

MATERIALS

LETTER	NUMBER REQUIRED	NAME	SIZE
A	1	HITCH	¼-inch dowel, 1½ inches long
B	1	FRONT SPACER	5 × 2½ × ½ inches
C	2	AXLE HOUSING	3⅝ × 4 × ¾ inches
D	8	AXLE	¼-inch dowel, 1½ inches long
E	8	WHEEL	1½ × 1½ × ¼ inches
F	4	WHEEL COVER	3⅝ × 1 × ¼ inches
G	1	REAR SPACER	2½ × 2½ × ½ inches
H	2	UPPER AND CENTER BEDS	15½ × 4½ × ½ inches
I	1	BOTTOM BED	17 × 4½ × ½ inches
J	6	DIAGONAL BRACE	9⅛ × ½ × ½ inches
K	8	UPRIGHT BRACE	8⅛ × ½ × ½ inches

Fifty 1-inch wire brads

TOOLS

Hammer
Ruler
Try square
Coping saw
Electric drill
Table saw
2½-inch hole saw
1¾-inch hole saw
¼-inch twist bit

CONSTRUCTION NOTES

Beds
Parts H and I

Use the table saw to cut part H, the upper and center beds. Use the coping saw and the table saw to cut part I, the bottom bed. Drill the hole for the hitch in part I, using a twist bit and an electric drill.

Braces
Parts J and K

Cut parts J and K with a table saw. After all the pieces for part K, the upright braces, have been cut, glue and nail (using wire brads) part K to the upper and center beds, part H, and the bottom bed, part I. Part K, the four braces at the ends of the auto carrier, should be flush with the ends of the beds. The tops of

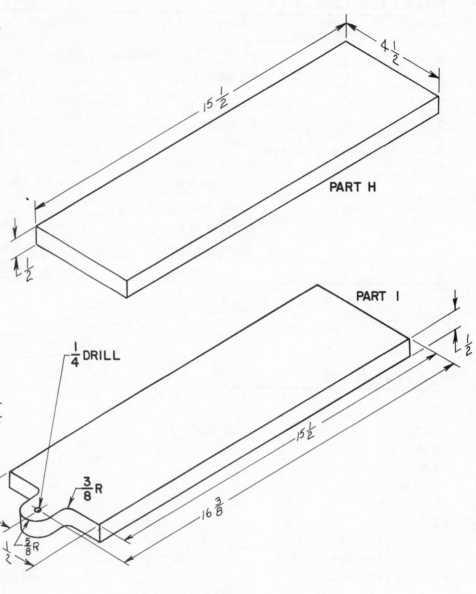

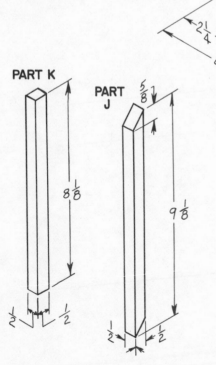

part K and the upper bed should be flush. The bottom of part K should be flush with the bottom of part I. The bottom of the center bed should be placed 3⅞ inches above the bottom of part I, the bottom bed. Attach the remaining four upright braces, part K, at equal intervals along the edge of parts H and I. Be sure parts H and I are square with part K, the upright braces.

Use a table saw to cut the correct angles on part J, the diagonal braces. Use a ½-inch square piece for part J. Glue and nail part J to parts H and I.

Axle Housing and Spacers Parts A, B, C, and G

Use a table saw to cut the axle housing, part C. Drill the holes with an electric drill and a twist bit. Cut part G, the rear spacer, with a 2½-inch hole saw. Glue and nail part G using wire brads, to the center of part C, the axle housing. Cut part B, the front spacer, using a coping saw. Drill the hole for the hitch with a twist bit and an electric drill. Glue and nail part B to part C, the axle housing, using wire brads. Part B should be centered on part C from side to side and should protrude in front by 2 inches.

Cut part A, the hitch, from a dowel rod using a coping saw. Glue it into part B with bottoms flush. Glue part B and part G to the bottom bed, part I. Keep the ends of part C flush with the ends of the bottom bed, part I, at both ends of the auto carrier.

Wheel and Axle Parts D, E, and F

Use a 1¾-inch hole saw and an electric drill to cut the wheels, part E. Next, cut the dowel for part D, the axle, to the size given using a coping saw. Resaw a piece of stock on the table saw to ¼-inch thickness for part F, the wheel cover. Cut part F with a coping saw. Drill the holes using a twist bit and an electric drill. Glue part D, the axle, into part C, the axle housing, so it protrudes ⅝ inch. Slide the wheels, part E, onto the axle, part D, making sure no glue gets on the wheels. Glue part F to the axles, part D, so the outsides of part D and part F are flush.

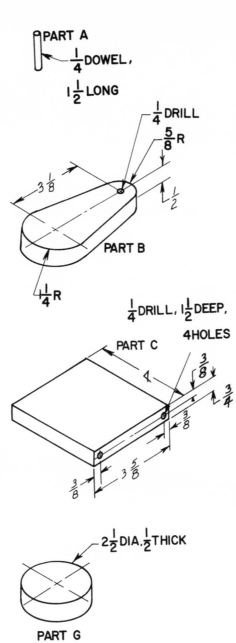

Auto

MATERIALS

LETTER	NUMBER REQUIRED	NAME	SIZE
A	1	BODY	6 × 3 × 1½ inches
B	2	AXLE	¼-inch dowel, 2⅜ inches long
C	4	WHEEL	1½ × 1½ × ½ inches

TOOLS

Jigsaw or band saw
Electric drill
1¾-inch hole saw
⅜-inch twist bit
1-inch Forstner bit
½-inch Forstner bit

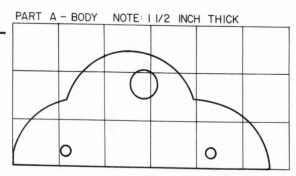

PART A – BODY   NOTE: 1 1/2 INCH THICK

NOTE: EACH SQUARE=1 INCH

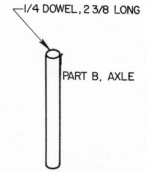

1/4 DOWEL, 2 3/8 LONG

PART B, AXLE

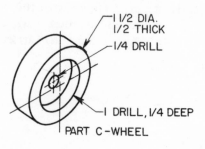

1 1/2 DIA.
1/2 THICK

1/4 DRILL

1 DRILL, 1/4 DEEP

PART C–WHEEL

CONSTRUCTION NOTES

Body
Part A

Cut part A, the body, from a 2-by-4 board with a jigsaw or a band saw. Drill the hole for the axle, using a ⅜-inch twist bit, and the hole for the window, using a ½-inch Forstner bit.

Wheel
Parts B and C

Cut part C, the wheels, using a hole saw and an electric drill. Drill the recessed portion of part C with a Forstner bit. Use a jig-saw or band saw to cut part B, the axle, to the correct length. Slide part B through the body, and glue the wheels to the axles. The wheels and axles should be flush on the outside.

Flat-Bed Car

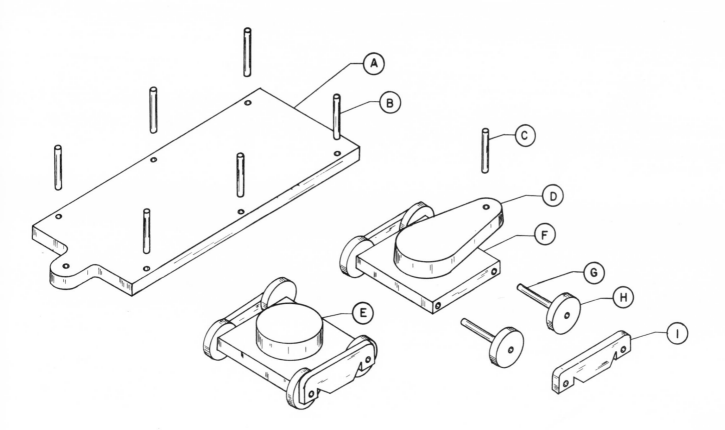

MATERIALS

LETTER	NUMBER REQUIRED	NAME	SIZE
A	1	BED	13½ × 4⅝ × ½ inches
B	6	STAKE	¼-inch dowel, 2½ inches long
C	1	HITCH	¼-inch dowel, 1½ inches long
D	1	FRONT SPACER	5⅜ × 2½ × ½ inches
E	1	BACK SPACER	2½ × 2½ × ½ inches
F	2	AXLE HOUSING	3⅜ × 4 × ¾ inches
G	8	AXLE	¼-inch dowel, 1½ inches long
H	8	WHEEL	1½ × 1½ × ¼ inches
I	4	WHEEL COVER	3⅜ × 1 × ¼ inches

Fifteen 1-inch wire brads

TOOLS

Try square
Ruler
Hammer
Hand screw or C-clamps
Coping saw
Table saw
Electric drill
2½-inch hole saw
1¾-inch hole saw
¼-inch twist bit

CONSTRUCTION NOTES

Bed
Parts A and B

Cut part A to the correct size using a table saw. Cut the curves on the end for the hitch, part C, using a coping saw. Lay out and drill the seven holes with an electric drill and twist bit. Cut out part B, the stakes, using a coping saw. Glue the stakes into the bed, part A, with bottoms flush.

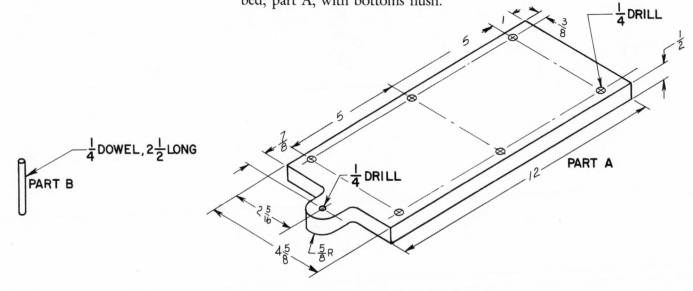

Axle Housing
Parts C, D, E, and F

Cut the axle housing, part F, with a table saw. Drill the holes with an electric drill and twist bit. Use a 2½-inch hole saw and an electric drill to cut part E, the back spacer. Glue and nail part E to part F using wire brads; center part E on part F.

Cut part D, the front spacer, with a coping saw. Drill the hole required for the hitch with an electric drill and twist bit. Glue part D, the front spacer, to part F, the axle housing, so part D is centered on part F from side to side and protrudes in front of part F by 2 inches. Cut part C, the hitch, using a coping saw. Glue part C into part D, with bottoms flush.

Glue and clamp part E, the back spacer, and part D, the front spacer, to part A, the bed, so the ends of the axle housing are flush with the ends of the bed.

Wheel
Parts G, H, and I

Cut the wheels, part H, with a 1¾-inch hole saw and an electric drill from a piece of ¼-inch re-sawed stock. Cut part I, the wheel cover, from a piece of ¼-inch resawed stock with a coping saw. Drill the holes in parts H and I with a twist bit and an electric drill. Cut the dowels for part G, the axle, using a coping saw. Glue part G into part F so the dowels protrude ⅝ inch. Slide the wheel on; do not permit glue to get on the wheel. Glue part I onto the axle so the outsides of part I and part G are flush.

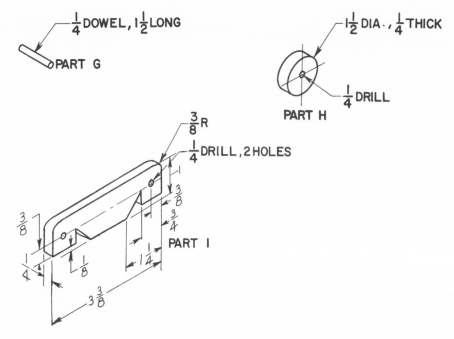

Gondola Car

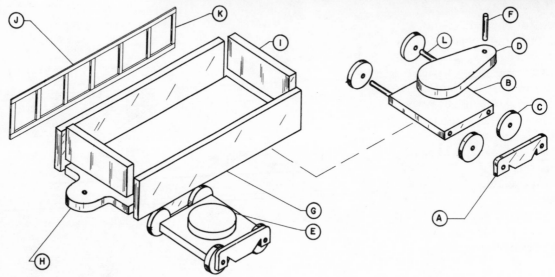

MATERIALS

LETTER	NUMBER REQUIRED	NAME	SIZE
A	4	WHEEL COVER	3⅝ × 1 × ¼ inches
B	2	AXLE HOUSING	3⅝ × 4 × ¾ inches
C	8	WHEEL	1½ × 1½ × ¼ inches
D	1	FRONT SPACER	5 × 2½ × ½ inches
E	1	BACK SPACER	2½ × 2½ × ½ inches
F	1	HITCH	¼-inch dowel, 1½ inches long
G	2	SIDE	11¾ × 2⁷/₁₆ × ⅜ inches
H	1	BOTTOM	12¼ × 4⅝ × ½ inches
I	2	END	4⅝ × 1¹⁵/₁₆ × ½ inches
J	4	HORIZONTAL TRIM	⅛ × ¼ × 11¾ inches
K	14	VERTICAL TRIM	⅛ × ¼ × 1¹⁵/₁₆ inches
L	8	AXLE	¼-inch dowel, 1⅝ inches long

Thirty ½-inch wire brads
Thirty 1-inch wire brads

TOOLS

Try square
Ruler
Compass
Hammer
Nail set
Table saw
Coping saw
Hand plane
Electric drill or drill press
Jointer
2½-inch hole saw
1¾-inch hole saw
¼-inch twist bit

CONSTRUCTION NOTES

Sides, Bottom, and Ends
Parts G, H, and I

Cut enough stock to make parts G, H, and I; either plane it with a jointer or hand plane or resaw it with a table saw. Cut part H, the bottom, using a table saw and coping saw. Drill the hole required for the hitch with a twist bit and an electric drill. Cut part G, the sides, and part I, the ends, using a table saw. Glue and nail with 1-inch wire brads part G to part H, so the bottom surfaces are flush. Glue and nail part I, the ends, to the side, part G, and the bottom, part H. Part I should be flush with the ends and top of part G.

Trim
Parts J and K

Cut the trim, parts J and K, using a table saw. Nail the horizontal trim, part J, to part G with ½-inch wire brads so that part J is flush with the top, bottom, and ends of the sides, part G. Glue and nail part K, the vertical trim, to the sides at equal intervals (approximately every 1¹⁵⁄₁₆ inches).

Axle Housing
Parts B, D, E, and F

Cut the axle housing, part B, using a table saw. Drill the holes using a ¼-inch twist bit and an electric drill. Cut part E, the

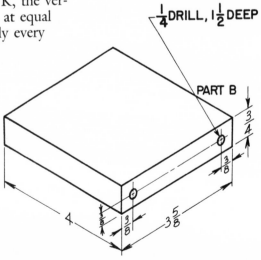

back spacer, using a hole saw
and an electric drill. Use a coping saw to cut part D, the front
spacer. Drill the hole using a ¼-
inch twist bit and an electric
drill. Use a coping saw to cut
part F, the hitch. Glue part F
into part D, keeping their bottoms flush. Glue and nail part E,
the back spacer, to the center of
part B, the axle housing, using
1-inch wire brads. Glue and nail
part D, the front spacer, to part
B, the axle housing, so that part
D is centered on part B from
side to side and protrudes in
front of part B 2 inches. Glue
the top of part E and part D to
the bottom of part H, the bottom; make sure that the end of
the rear axle housing is even
with the square portion of the
end of the bottom.

Wheel
Parts A, C, and L

Cut the wheels, part C, using a
hole saw and an electric drill.
Cut the dowel rod for part L,
the axle, using a coping saw. Use
a table saw and a coping saw to
cut part A. Glue part L into part
B so the axle protrudes from the
axle housing by ⅝ inch. Slide
the wheels onto the axle. *Do not
glue.* Glue part A onto part L,
keeping the ends of the axle
flush with the outside of part A.

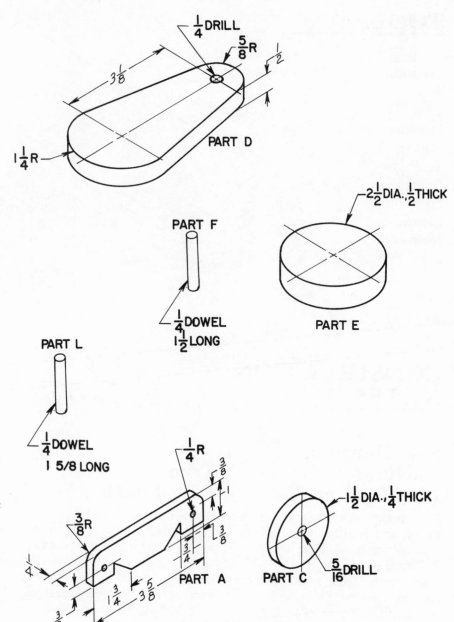

Tanker Car

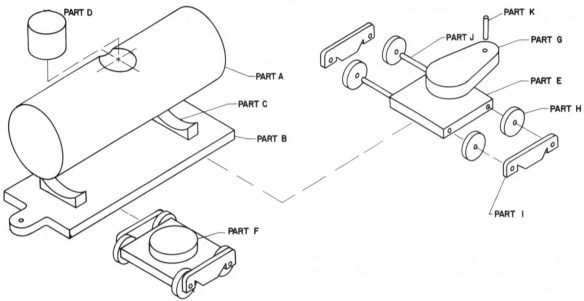

MATERIALS

LETTER	NUMBER REQUIRED	NAME	SIZE
A	1	TANK	4 × 4 × 12 inches
B	1	BED	13¼ × 4⅝ × ½ inches
C	2	TANK SUPPORT	2½ × ¾ × ¾ inches
D	1	TANK CAP	2 × 2 × 1½ inches
E	2	AXLE HOUSING	3⅝ × 4 × ¾ inches
F	1	BACK SPACER	2½ × 2½ × ½ inches
G	1	FRONT SPACER	5 × 2½ × ½ inches
H	8	WHEEL	1½ × 1½ × ¼ inches
I	4	WHEEL COVER	3⅝ × 1 × ¼ inches
J	8	AXLE	¼-inch dowel, 2 inches long
K	1	HITCH	¼-inch dowel, 1½ inches long

Two 1¼ × 10 flat head wood
 screws

53

TOOLS

Try square
Ruler
Hammer
Standard screwdriver
Hand screw clamps or C-clamps
Coping saw
Table saw
Wood lathe
Electric drill
2-inch spade bit
2½-inch hole saw
1¾-inch hole saw
¼-inch twist bit
5/16-inch twist bit

CONSTRUCTION NOTES

Axle Housing
Parts E, F, G, and K

Cut the axle housing, part E, on a table saw. Drill the holes for part J, the axle, using an electric drill and a ¼-inch twist bit. Using a table saw, resaw enough stock to a ½-inch thickness to make parts F and G. Cut part F, the back spacer, using an electric drill and a hole saw. Part G, the front spacer, should be cut with a coping saw. Drill the hole using an electric drill and a twist bit. Cut part K, the hitch, from a dowel rod with a coping saw. Assemble part F and part E by gluing and clamping; center part F on part E. Glue and clamp part G to part E so part G is centered on part E from side to side and protrudes 2 inches in front. Glue part K into part G, with bottoms flush.

Tank
Parts A and D

Turn the tank, part A, on the wood lathe. Drill the hole for part D, the tank cap, using a spade bit and an electric drill. Turn part D on the wood lathe; it should fit firmly in the hole drilled in the tank, part A. Glue part D into part A.

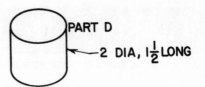

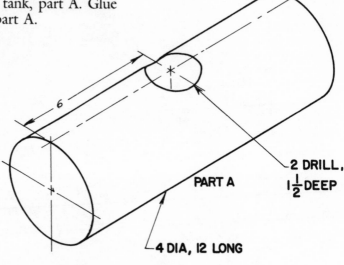

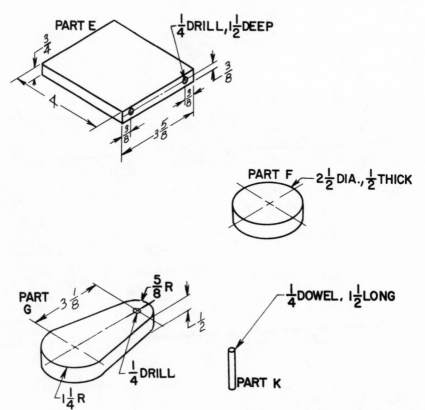

Bed
Parts B and C

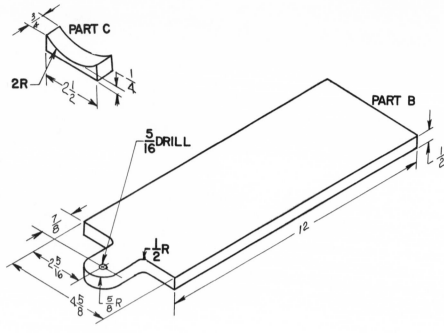

Using a table saw, cut out part B, the bed, to its overall size. A coping saw can be used to cut the curved section for the hitch. Drill the hole required using an electric drill and a 5/16-inch twist bit. Cut part C, the tank supports, using a coping saw. To assemble parts A, B, and C place the tank, part A, on the tank supports, part C. The tank supports should be placed 1½ inches from each end of the tank. Place the tank and tank supports on the bed; the ends of bed and tank should be flush, except for the section of the bed that protrudes for the hitch. Use an electric drill to drill a hole from the bottom of the bed, part B, through part B and part C, the tank supports, and into the tank, part A. Drive a wood screw into this hole with a standard screwdriver; parts A, B, and C will be attached firmly.

Wheel
Parts H, I, and J

Resaw a piece of stock to ¼-inch thickness on a table saw for the wheels, part H. Using an electric drill and a hole saw, cut the wheels. Cut the axles, part J, from a dowel rod with a coping saw. Also use a coping saw to cut part I; drill the holes with an electric drill and a ¼-inch twist bit. Glue the axles, part J, into the axle housing, part E, with the axles protruding 5/8 inch. Slide the wheels, part H, onto the axle. Make sure no glue is on the wheels: glue would prevent them from turning. Glue part I onto the axle, part J, leaving the ends of part J flush on the outside of part I.

Once parts E, F, G, K, J, H, and I are assembled in one unit glue and clamp part F, the back spacer, and part G, the front spacer, to the bottom of the bed, part B. The axle housing should be flush with the ends of the tank.

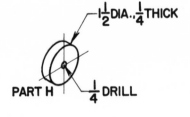

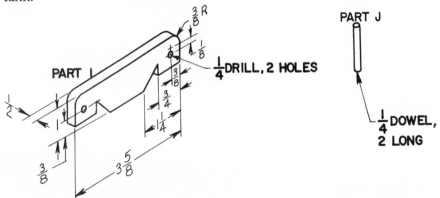

Caboose

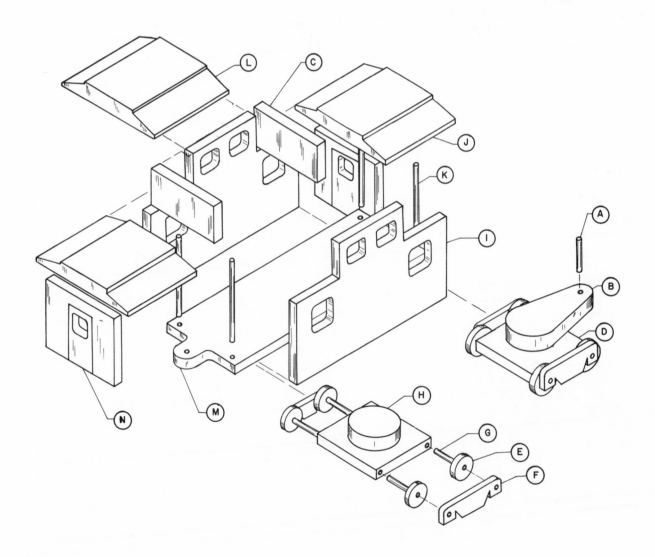

MATERIALS

LETTER	NUMBER REQUIRED	NAME	SIZE
A	1	HITCH	¼-inch dowel, 1½ inches long
B	1	FRONT SPACER	5 × 2½ × ½ inches
C	2	END, TOP SECTION	4⅝ × 2 × ½ inches
D	2	AXLE HOUSING	3⅝ × 4 × ¾ inches
E	8	WHEEL	1½ × 1½ × ¼ inches
F	4	WHEEL COVER	3⅝ × 1 × ¼ inches
G	8	AXLE	¼-inch dowel, 1½ inches long
H	1	BACK SPACER	2½ × 2½ × ½ inches
I	2	SIDE	6½ × 10 × ½ inches
J	2	LOWER TOP	6¼ × 4¾ × ¾ inches
K	4	POST	¼-inch dowel, 4¾ inches long
L	1	UPPER TOP	6¼ × 4⅜ × ¾ inches
M	1	BOTTOM	14½ × 4⅝ × ½ inches
N	2	END	4 × 4⅝ × ½ inches

Thirty 1-inch wire brads

TOOLS

Try square
Ruler
Compass
Hammer
Hand plane
Nail set
Knife
Vise
Coping saw
Table saw
Drill press or electric drill
Jointer
2½-inch hole saw
1¾-inch hole saw
¼-inch twist bit

CONSTRUCTION NOTES

Bottom, Side, and Ends Parts C, I, M, and N

Use a hand plane, a jointer, or a table saw to plane or resaw enough stock to make parts M, N, C, and I. Cut part M, the bottom, using a table saw and a coping saw. Drill the 5 holes with a twist bit and an electric drill. Cut the side, part I, using a table saw and a coping saw. Part N, the ends, should also be cut with a coping saw and a table saw. Carve the grooves that outline the door with a knife. Use a table saw to cut the end, top section, part C.

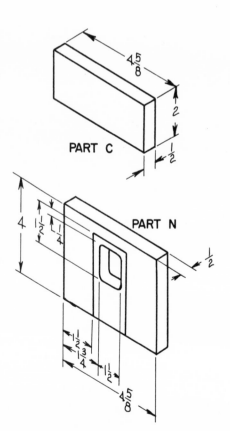

Glue and nail the sides, part I, to the bottom, part M, with bottoms flush. Place the sides 1½ inches from the square end portions of part M. Glue and nail the ends, part N, to the bottom, part M, keeping them flush with the end of the sides, part I. The tops of part I and part N should also be flush. Glue and nail part C, the end top section, to the sides, part I, with the outside and the top of each part flush.

Tops and Post Parts J, K, and L

Cut part J, the lower top, and part L, the upper top, using one 15-inch-long piece of stock. Cut the bevel (see the chapter titled Helpful Hints), then cut the individual pieces for the top with a table saw. Glue and nail part L, the upper top, to the top of the sides, part I, and the end, top section, part C, leaving a ¼-inch overhang on all sides. Drill two ¼-inch-deep holes with a twist bit in the bottom of part J, 1⅜ inches in from the side and ¼ inch in from the outside end. Glue and nail part J, the lower top, to each end so part J sits on the side, part I, and the end, part N, as shown in the photograph. Slide part K, the post, through the holes in part M and part J and glue part K into parts J and M.

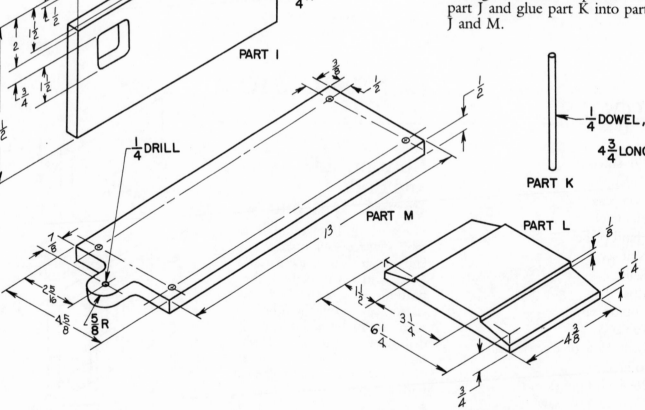

NOTE: PART J IS EXACTLY THE SAME AS PART L WITH ONE EXCEPTION THE LENGTH OF 4 3/8 IS 4 3/4 ON PART J.

Axle Housing
Parts A, B, D, and H

Using a table saw cut part D, the axle housing. Drill the four holes 1 inch deep with a twist bit and an electric drill. Cut part H, the back spacer, using a hole saw and an electric drill. Use a coping saw to cut part B, the front spacer; use an electric drill and a twist bit to drill the hole. Cut part A, the hitch, from a dowel rod. Glue part A into part B, with bottoms flush. Glue and nail part B, the front spacer, to part D, the axle housing, centering part B from side to side and letting it protrude past part D 2 inches. Glue and nail part H to the center of part D. Glue the top of part H, the back spacer, and the top of part B, the front spacer, to the bottom of part M, the bottom. The ends of part D should be flush with the square portion of part M, the bottom.

Wheel
Parts E, F, and G

Cut part E, the wheels, using a hole saw and an electric drill. Cut the axles, part G, with a coping saw; use a table saw and a coping saw to cut part F, the wheel cover. Use an electric drill and a twist bit to drill the holes in parts E and F. Glue the axles, part G, into the axle housing, part D, so part G protrudes ⅝ inch. Slide the wheels, part E, onto the axles, part G. *Do not glue.* Glue part F onto part G, with outside surfaces flush.

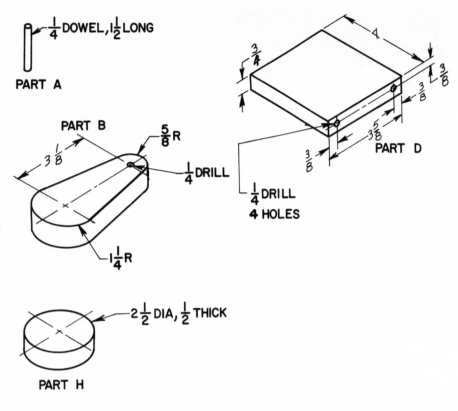

Three-Wheel Motorcycle

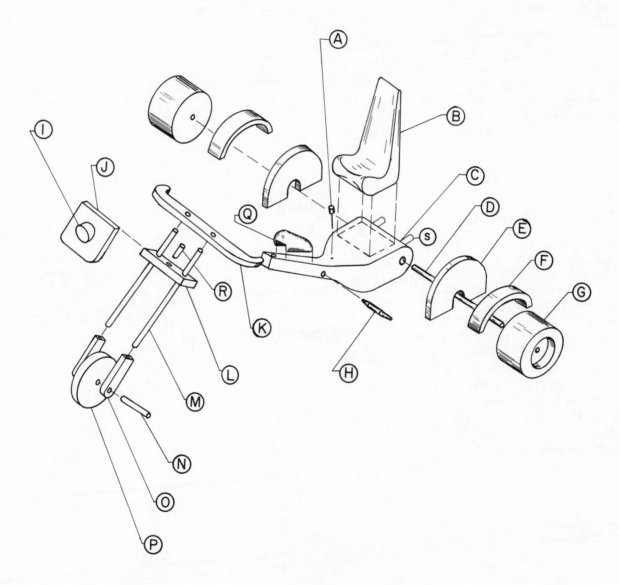

MATERIALS

LETTER	NUMBER REQUIRED	NAME	SIZE
A	1	GEAR SHIFT KNOB	¼-inch dowel, ¼ inch long
B	1	SEAT	4½ × 3½ × 2 inches
C	1	FRAME	7½ × 3½ × 3 inches
D	1	BACK AXLE	¼-inch dowel, 5½ inches long
E	2	FENDER SUPPORT	3½ × 1¾ × ¼ inches
F	2	FENDER	¾ × 3½ × 1¾ inches
G	2	BACK WHEEL	2½ × 2½ × 1½ inches
H	1	FOOTREST	¼-inch dowel, 1⅝ inches long
I	1	HEADLIGHT	¾-inch dowel, ½ inch long
J	1	HEADLIGHT BRACKET	2 × 1¾ × ⅛ inches
K	1	HANDLEBARS	5½ × 1½ × ¼ inches
L	1	FRONT FORK SUPPORT	2¼ × ⅝ × ½ inches
M	2	FRONT FORK	¼-inch dowel, 5½ inches long
N	1	FRONT AXLE	¼-inch dowel, 1⅜ inches long
O	2	WHEEL BRACKET	1¹¹⁄₁₆ × ⅝ × ⅜ inches
P	1	FRONT WHEEL	2½ × 2½ × ¼ inches
Q	1	GAS TANK	1¾-inch round molding, 2 inches long
R	1	PIVOT POST	¼-inch dowel, 1 inch long
S	2	TAIL PIPE	¼-inch dowel, 1 inch long

Two 1-inch wire brads

TOOLS

Try square
Ruler
Clamps
Hammer
Wood file
Wood chisel
Pliers
Coping saw
Table saw
Band saw
½-inch electric drill

⁵⁄₁₆-inch twist bit
¼-inch twist bit
¹⁄₁₆-inch twist bit
2½-inch hole saw
1½-inch Forstner bit

CONSTRUCTION NOTES

Frame and Seat Parts C and B

Laminate two pieces of 2-by-4 stock to the size indicated. Drill the hole for the back axle, part D, using a ⁵⁄₁₆-inch twist bit and an electric drill. Drill the two holes for part S, the tail pipe, using a ¼-inch twist bit and an electric drill.

Cut part C to the contours shown on the side view and the top view using a band saw. Drill a ¼-inch hole for part H, the footrest, and a ¼-inch hole for part R, the pivot post, using a twist bit and an electric drill.

Cut part B, the seat, using a band saw. Glue the bottom of part B to part C, as shown in the illustration.

TOP VIEW

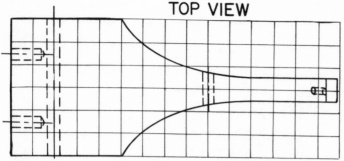

PART C   NOTE: EACH SQUARE = $\frac{1}{2}$ INCH

SIDE VIEW

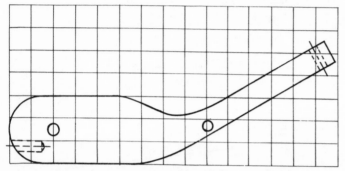

PART B — NOTE: EACH SQUARE = $\frac{1}{2}$ INCH

LEFT SIDE VIEW

FRONT VIEW

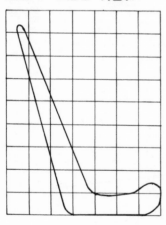

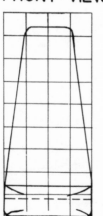

Gas Tank, Gear Shift Knob, Footrest, and Tail Pipe Parts A, H, Q, and S

Use a piece of round molding to make part Q, the gas tank. Carve the groove on the bottom with a wood file or wood chisel. Round the gas tank on each end with a wood file, and sand. Part Q, the gas tank, should fit firmly over part C, the frame. Glue part Q to part C so part Q is 1 inch from the front end of part C. Using a coping saw, cut the dowel rod for part H, the footrest. Taper the ends slightly by sanding. Glue part H, the footrest, into the frame, part C, leaving approximately ½ inch of part H protruding on each side of part C.

Cut the gear shift knob, part A, using a coping saw. Round the end slightly, using sandpaper. Drill a ¹⁄₁₆-inch hole halfway through one end of the gear shift knob. Drive a wire brad into the frame, part C, about ⅞ inch in front of the seat and in the center of part C from side to side. Cut the head off the wire brad, using a pair of pliers with side cutters. Glue the gear shift knob, part A, onto the brad.

Cut part S, the tail pipe, using a coping saw. Glue part S into the holes in part C, leaving part S protruding from part C ¼ inch.

$\frac{1}{2}$DIA, 2 LONG

PART Q

$\frac{3}{8}$ ROUND MOLDING

DADO $\frac{1}{2}$ WIDE, $\frac{1}{2}$ DEEP

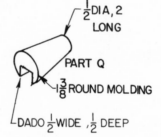

PART O

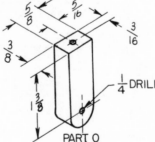

PART A - $\frac{1}{4}$ DOWEL, $\frac{1}{4}$ LONG

PART S - $\frac{1}{4}$ DOWEL, 1 LONG

PART D - $\frac{1}{4}$ DOWEL, 5$\frac{1}{2}$ LONG

PART M - $\frac{1}{4}$ DOWEL, 5$\frac{1}{2}$ LONG

PART N - $\frac{1}{4}$ DOWEL, 1$\frac{3}{8}$ LONG

PART R - $\frac{1}{4}$ DOWEL, 1 LONG

45°

$\frac{3}{4}$ DOWEL, $\frac{1}{2}$ LONG

PART I

PART H - $\frac{1}{4}$ DOWEL, 1$\frac{5}{8}$ LONG, TAPERED

AS SHOWN IN EXPLODED VIEW

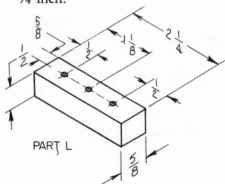

PART L

Back Fender
Parts E and F

Cut part E, the fender support, and part F, the fender, with a coping saw or band saw. Glue and clamp the fender, part F, to the fender support, part E, so the tops are flush and there is approximately a ½-inch space from the bottom of part E to the bottom of part F. Glue part E and part F as one unit to the frame, part C, so the bottom of the fender support, part E, is ⅝ inch from the bottom of the frame, part C.

Back Wheel
and Axle
Parts D and G

Using a hole saw and an electric drill cut the back wheels, part G. Drill the center portion out with a Forstner bit and an electric drill. Cut the dowel rod to length for the axle, part D. Slide the axle, part D, through the hole on part C, the frame. Glue the back wheels, part G, to the axles, part D, so part D is flush with the outside of part G.

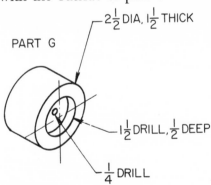

Handlebars
Parts K, L, M, O, and R

Using a coping saw or band saw, cut the handlebars, part K. Drill the two ¼-inch holes for part M

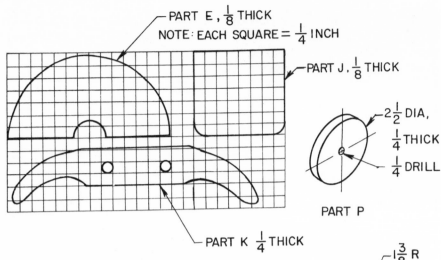

with a ¼-inch twist bit and an electric drill. Cut a dowel rod to the correct lengths for parts M and R with a coping saw. Cut part L on the table saw; drill the three holes with a ¼-inch twist bit and an electric drill. Cut part O, the wheel bracket, with a table saw and a coping saw. Drill the ¼-inch hole for part M and drill the hole for the axle, part N, using an electric drill and a twist bit.

To assemble these parts, put a drop of glue in the three holes in part L. Glue part R in the center hole, with tops flush. Slide part M into part L so part M protrudes 2 inches above part L. Glue the handlebars, part K, onto part M, with tops flush. Glue part O to part M, making sure the two axle holes line up: the bottom of part O should be 6¾ inches from the top of the handlebars, part K. Slide part R onto the hole in the frame, part C. This should fit snugly, allowing the handlebars to turn.

Front Wheel
and Axle
Parts N and P

Cut part N, the front axle, using a coping saw. Resaw a piece of lumber to the correct thickness

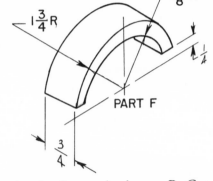

for the front wheel, part P. Cut the wheel, part P, using a hole saw and an electric drill. Put a drop of glue in each of the axle holes in part O. Slide part N, the front axle, through one of the two pieces of part O, through the wheel, part P, and then through the second piece of part O. The axle, part N, should be flush on the outside with part O. No glue is applied to the wheel, allowing part P to turn.

Headlight
Parts I and J

Cut part J, the headlight bracket, and part I, the headlight, on the band saw. Glue part I to part J, ¼ inch from the top of part J and ⅝ inch from either side. Glue part J to part L, keeping the tops flush. There should be ⅛ inch of part L extending on both sides of part J.

Motorcycle

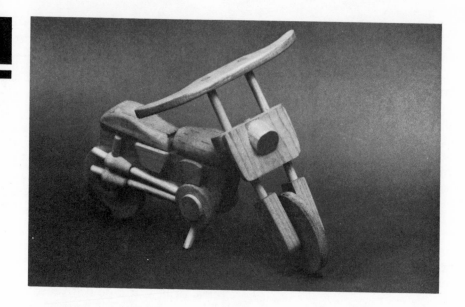

MATERIALS

LETTER	NUMBER REQUIRED	NAME	SIZE
A	1	GAS TANK	1⅜-inch round molding, 2 inches long
B	1	SEAT	2¾ × 1 × ¾ inches
C	1	FRAME	6½ × 4 × ¾ inches
D	2	WHEEL	2½ × 2½ × ¼ inches
E	2	SHOCK ABSORBER	¼-inch dowel, cut to fit
F	4	TAIL PIPE	¼-inch dowel, ½ inch long
G	1	REAR AXLE	¼-inch dowel, ¾ inch long
H	4	HEADER PIPE	¼-inch dowel, 1¾ inches long
I	2	ENGINE	1⅛ × 1⅛ × 3/16 inches
J	1	KICKSTAND	¼-inch dowel, 1½ inches long
K	2	TRIM	1⅛ × ¾ × ⅛ inches thick
L	2	ENGINE COVER	¾-inch dowel, ⅛ inch long
M	2	CYLINDER HEAD	¾ × ¾ × ⅛ inches thick
N	1	FRONT AXLE	¼-inch dowel, ½ inch long
O	4	MUFFLER	⅜-inch dowel, ½ inch long
P	2	WHEEL BRACKET	1 21/32 × 7/16 × 11/16 inches
Q	1	HEADLIGHT	¾-inch dowel, ½ inch long
R	1	HEADLIGHT BRACKET	2 × 1½ × 5/32 inches
S	2	FRONT FORK	¼-inch dowel, 4 inches long
T	1	HANDLEBARS	5½ × 1¼ × ¼ inches
U	1	PIVOT POST	⅛-inch dowel, 1 inch long
V	1	FRONT FORK SUPPORT	2¼ × ⅝ × 7/16 inches

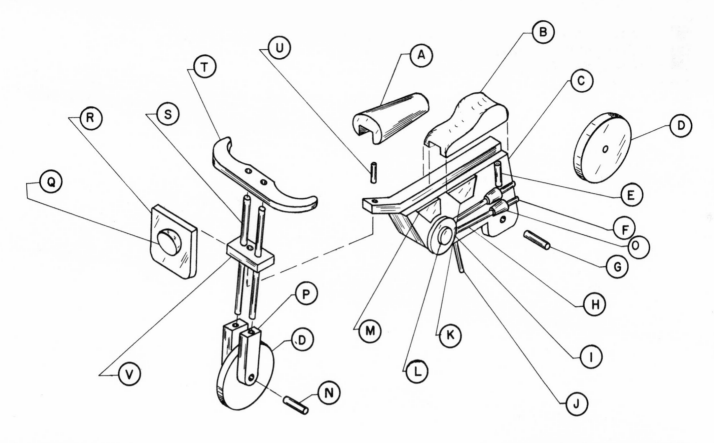

TOOLS

Try square	Band saw
Wood file	Jigsaw
Vise	Belt sander
Clamps	Electric drill
Coping saw	2½-inch hole saw
Ruler	¼-inch twist bit
Table saw	

NOTE: EACH SQUARE = ½ INCH

PART C - THICKNESS IS 3/4, 1/2 AT AREA SHOWN

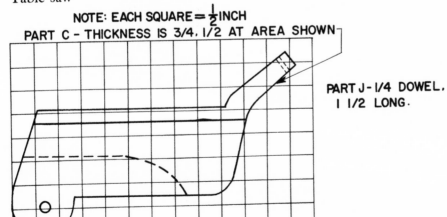

PART J - 1/4 DOWEL, 1 1/2 LONG.

CONSTRUCTION NOTES

Frame and Kickstand Parts C and J

Cut the grooves on the top portion of part C, the frame, with a table saw. Cut two or three saw kerfs to make a groove ⁵⁄₁₆ inch wide to accommodate the back wheel, part D. This groove is shown by a dashed line on the drawing of the frame. Using an electric drill and ¼-inch twist bit, drill the hole for part U, the pivot post. Lay out the shape of part C, the frame, then drill the ¼-inch hole for the rear axle, part G, using a ¼-inch twist bit and an electric drill. Drill the ¼-inch hole in the bottom of the frame for the kickstand, part J; this hole should be 3⅞ inches from the rear of the motorcycle. Cut the frame of the motorcycle, using a band saw.

Seat and Gas Tank Parts A and B

Cut part A, the gas tank, from a piece of round molding using the table saw. File the groove in the bottom of part A with a wood file; use the wood file to round off both ends. Glue part A, the gas tank, to part C, the frame, with fronts as close to flush as possible. Cut out part B, the seat, using a coping saw. File the groove with a wood file and round the seat with the wood file and sandpaper. Glue the seat, part B, to the frame, part C, just behind the gas tank, part A, so the backs of part B and part C are flush.

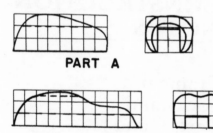

PART A

PART B

NOTE: EACH SQUARE = $\frac{1}{4}$ INCH

Cylinder Head, Trim, Engine, and Engine Cover Parts I, K, L, and M

Cut part M, the cylinder head, and part K, the trim, using either a jigsaw or a coping saw, from a piece of resawed stock. Glue and clamp part M, the cylinder head, so it reaches the bottom of the gas tank, part A, and

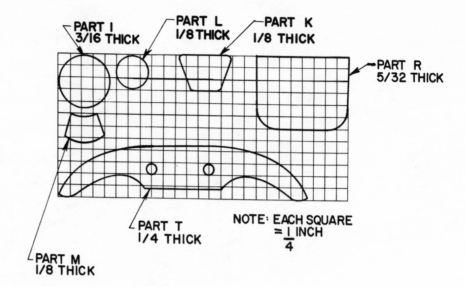

PART I 3/16 THICK

PART L 1/8 THICK

PART K 1/8 THICK

PART R 5/32 THICK

PART T 1/4 THICK

PART M 1/8 THICK

NOTE: EACH SQUARE = $\frac{1}{4}$ INCH

is ¾ inch from the front of the frame, part C. Glue and clamp part K, the trim, so it is ⅜ inch from part M, the cylinder head, and flush with the notched cut on the frame, part C.

Cut part I, the engine, and part L, the engine cover, on a band saw. Glue and clamp part I, the engine, so that it fits snugly under part M, the cylinder head. Glue and clamp the engine cover, part L, to the center of the engine, part I.

Header Pipe, Muffler, Tail Pipe, and Shock Absorber Parts E, F, H, and O

Using a belt sander, sand a 14-inch-long dowel rod flat on one side, making it a half-cylinder shape. Cut part H, the header pipe, part F, the tail pipe, and part E, the shock absorber, from the dowel rod, using a coping saw. Sand flat on one side a ⅜-inch dowel rod that is 4 inches long. Cut off the pieces needed for the muffler, part O, using a coping saw. Sand the tapered

portion of one end and round the other, using a medium grade sandpaper.

Glue and clamp part H, the header pipes, so they touch each other at the engine. The bottom header is ⅛ inch from the bottom of the frame, part C; the top header is ¼ to ½ inch above the bottom header pipe, as shown in the photograph.

Glue and clamp the muffler, part O, so it is centered behind part H and touches part H. Line up the center of the tail pipe, part F, with parts O and H; glue and clamp part F so it touches the muffler and hangs over the end of the frame, part C, ⅛ inch. Part E, the shock absorber, should be glued and clamped so it touches the muffler on the bottom and the seat on the top. It should be parallel to the end of the frame, part C, and ¾ inch from the end of the frame.

Wheel and Axle Parts D, G, and N

Make part D, the wheels, by resawing a piece of stock on the table saw. Cut the wheels with a hole saw and an electric drill.

PART E- 1/4 DOWEL, CUT DOWN THE CENTER.
PART F- 1/4 DOWEL, 1/2 LONG, CUT AS ABOVE.
PART H- 1/4 DOWEL, 1 3/4 LONG, CUT AS ABOVE.
PARTS N & G- 1/4 DOWEL, 3/4 LONG.
PART S- 1/4 DOWEL, 4 LONG.
PART U- 1/8 DOWEL OR METAL ROD, 1 LONG.

3/8 DOWEL, 1/2 LONG
5/16 DIA.
PART O

2 1/2 DIA., 1/4 THICK
PART D
1/4 DRILL

45°
PART Q
3/4 DOWEL.

1/2   1 1/8   2 1/4
5/16
1/4 DRILL
PART V
7/16
5/8

11/16   7/32
11/32   7/16
1 5/16
1/4 DRILL
PART P
1/4 DRILL
11/32 R

Cut a dowel rod for part G, the rear axle, and part N, the front axle. Put a drop of glue in both back axle holes of the frame, part C. Slide the rear axle, part G, through one hole, through the wheel, and through the second hole in the frame. The rear axle, part G, should be flush with the frame on both sides. Be sure not to glue the wheel; it should turn freely after a little use. Part N will be assembled later.

Note: If the motorcycle is to be fitted with the Sidecar, see the motorcycle Sidecar construction notes before gluing part G, the rear axle.

Handlebars, Front Fork, Front Fork Support, Wheel Bracket, Pivot Post, and Front Axle Parts N, P, S, T, U, and V

Cut the handlebars, part T, using a jigsaw or coping saw. Drill the two holes in part T for part S with a ¼-inch twist bit and an electric drill. Cut part S, the front fork, and part U, the pivot post, with a coping saw. The wheel bracket, part P, and front fork support, part V, should be cut with a jigsaw or a band saw. Drill the three holes in part V and the three holes in part P, using an electric drill and twist bit. Place a drop of glue in each of the holes in part V. Slide part U, the pivot post, into the middle holes of part V so the tops are flush. Slide part S into the two holes on part V so they protrude from the top of part V by 1⁷⁄₁₆ inch. Glue the handlebars, part T, onto part S, keeping the tops flush. Glue part P to the bottom of part S, the front fork, so the bottom of part P is 5¼ inches from the top of the handlebars, part T. Be sure the two holes for the front axle in part P are exactly aligned. Insert the wheel, part D, between the two wheel brackets. Slide part N, the front axle, through the hole in part P, through part D, and through the second hole in part P; the axle should be flush with the outside of P on both sides. Glue part N to part P but do not let the glue touch the wheel.

Headlight and Headlight Bracket Parts Q and R

Cut part R using a coping saw. Cut part Q from a dowel rod using a table saw. Glue part Q to part R so part Q is centered on part R. Glue part R to part V so their tops are flush and part R is centered on part V from side to side.

Sidecar

MATERIALS

LETTER	NUMBER REQUIRED	NAME	SIZE
A	1	WINDSHIELD	1½ × 1½ × approximately ³⁄₃₂ inches, Plexiglas
B	1	SUPPORT	¼-inch dowel, 2⅛ inches long
C	1	BODY	4½ × 2 × 2½ inches
D	1	AXLE	¼-inch dowel, 4¼ inches long
E	1	FENDER	2¾ × 1 × ¾ inches
F	1	WHEEL	2¼ × 2¼ × ¼ inches
G	1	HUB	¾-inch dowel, ⅜ inch long

TOOLS

Mallet or hammer
Try square
Ruler
Wood chisel
Belt or disk sander
Band saw
Table saw
½-inch electric drill
2½-inch hole saw
1-inch Forstner bit
1½-inch Forstner bit
¼-inch twist bit
⁵⁄₁₆-inch twist bit

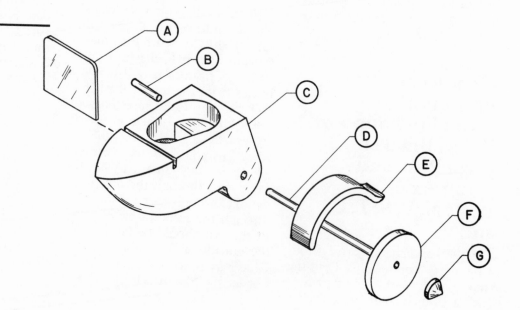

CONSTRUCTION NOTES

Body and Support Parts B and C

Lay out the shape of part C, the body, and cut a saw kerf for the windshield, part A, using a table saw. This should be done from a board 12 inches or longer to ensure a safe operation. Drill the 1-inch hole, using a Forstner bit, for the deepest portion of the seat area. Then drill the 1½-inch hole and use a wood chisel to carve the straight portion between the two holes. Cut the shape on a band saw, as shown in the front view. Drill the hole for the axle with a ¼-inch twist bit and an electric drill. Drill the hole for the support, part B, with a twist bit and an electric drill. With the band saw cut the contour shown on the top view.

Cut the support, part B, with a band saw and glue it into the hole on the frame, part C.

PART C

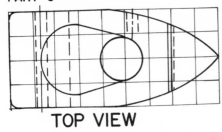

TOP VIEW

NOTE: EACH SQUARE = ½ INCH

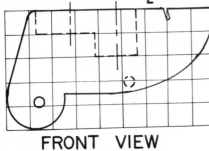

FRONT VIEW

PART B - ¼ DOWEL, 2⅛ LONG

Fender Part E

Cut the fender, part E, using a band saw. Glue and clamp part E to the body so it protrudes from the back of the body by 1¼ inches and is ⅛ inch below the top of the body.

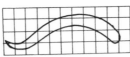

PART E, THICKNESS IS ¾ INCH

Wheel, Axle, and Hub Parts D, F, and G

Cut the axle, part D, using a band saw. This axle replaces the small axle on the motorcycle and passes through the sidecar and the motorcycle. Glue the axle, part D, into the frame of the motorcycle, leaving about ⅞ inch between the motorcycle and the sidecar. Cut part F, the wheel, using an electric drill and hole saw. Slide the wheel over the axle, making sure there is no glue on it. Make the hub, part G, by sanding the end of a dowel rod to a cone shape with a belt or disk sander or by hand. Cut the dowel rod to the correct length using the band saw. Drill the hole ¼ inch deep with a twist bit. Glue the hub, part G, to the end of the axle, part D.

PART F

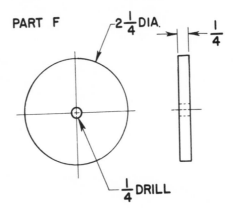

2¼ DIA.

¼

¼ DRILL

PART D - ¼ DOWEL, 4¼ LONG

BECOMES MOTORCYCLE BACK AXLE AS WELL AS SIDECAR AXLE.

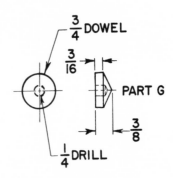

¾ DOWEL

3/16

PART G

⅜

¼ DRILL

Windshield Part A

Use a piece of Plexiglas 1/16 to 3/32 inch thick for the windshield, part A. Cut the windshield on the band saw and sand the edges smooth with a fine piece of sandpaper. Gently tap the windshield, part A, into the saw kerf on part C until it reaches the bottom of the kerf. Gluing is not necessary.

PART A

3/32 PLEXIGLAS THICKNESS

NOTE: EACH SQUARE = ¼ INCH

Tank

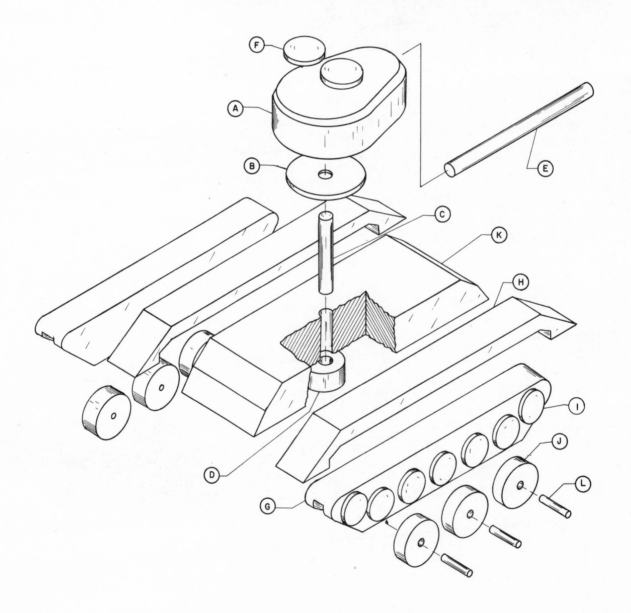

MATERIALS

LETTER	NUMBER REQUIRED	NAME	SIZE
A	1	CAPSULE	5¼ × 3½ × 1¾ inches
B	1	SPACER	2⅜ × 2⅜ × 3⁄16 inches
C	1	POLE	½-inch dowel, 3 inches long
D	1	WASHER	1¾-inch round molding, ½ inch long
E	1	BARREL	½-inch dowel, 7 inches long
F	2	HATCH	1¾-inch round molding, ¼ inch long
G	2	TRACKS	10½ × 2 × 1½ inches
H	2	FENDER	12¾ × 1⅛ × 1 7⁄16 inches
I	14	ROLLER	1⅜-inch round molding, ⅛ inch long
J	6	HIDDEN WHEEL	1½ × 1½ × 7⁄16 inches
K	1	BODY	11⅛ × 3½ × 1½ inches
L	6	AXLE	¼-inch dowel, 1⅛ inches long

Four No. 8 finishing nails

TOOLS

Try square	Ruler
Hammer	Table saw
Nail set	Electric drill
Coping saw	Jigsaw
Clamps	½-inch spade bit
File	1¾-inch hole saw
Compass	2½-inch hole saw

CONSTRUCTION NOTES

Body and Fender Parts H and K

Cut part K, the body, from a 2-by-6 piece of stock, using a table saw. Drill the hole with an electric drill and a spade bit. Cut part H, the fender, with a table saw and a jigsaw. Glue and clamp the fenders, part H, to part K, the body, keeping the tops flush. Part H should be 13⁄16 inch longer than part K on each end.

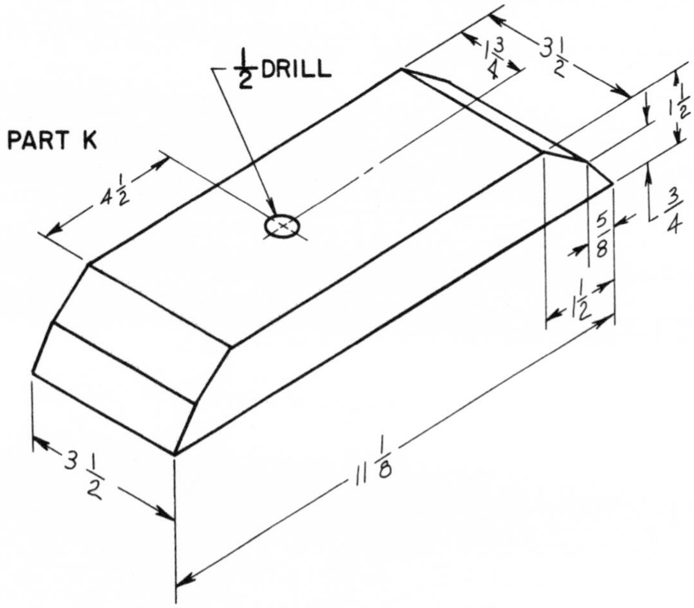

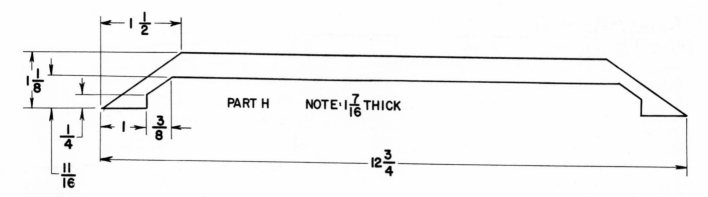

PART H   NOTE: $1\frac{7}{16}$ THICK

Tracks and Roller Parts G and I

The tracks, part G, should be cut using a table saw; cut the dado on the table saw also. Cut the shape required on a jigsaw. Drill the three ¼-inch holes with a twist bit and an electric drill. Attach part G, the tracks, to the body, part K, using two finishing nails. Part G should be ⅛ inch below part H, the fenders, and centered from end to end. Cut part I, the roller, from a piece of round molding; it will be attached later.

PART I — $1\frac{3}{8}$ ROUND MOLDING, $\frac{1}{8}$ LONG

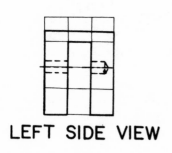

LEFT SIDE VIEW

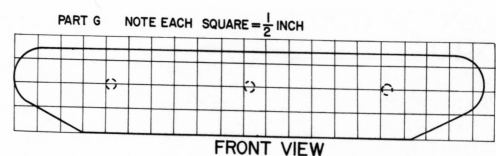

PART G   NOTE EACH SQUARE = $\frac{1}{2}$ INCH

FRONT VIEW

Hidden Wheel
Parts J and L

Cut part J, the hidden wheels, using a 1¾-inch hole saw. Cut the axle, part L, using a coping saw. Place a drop of glue in the three holes on part G, the tracks. Slide the axles, part L, into the holes on the tracks, part G, and through the holes in the hidden wheels, part J. Do not allow glue on the hidden wheels, part J.

Glue the rollers, part I, on the tracks, part G, spacing them ⅛ inch apart and about ¼ inch from the bottom of part G, the tracks.

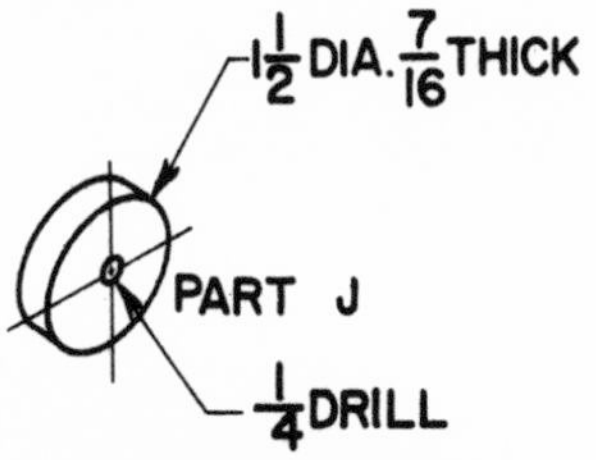

1½ DIA. $\frac{7}{16}$ THICK

PART J

¼ DRILL

PART L — ¼ DOWEL, 1⅛ LONG

Barrel
Parts A, E, and F

Cut part E, the barrel, using a jigsaw. Cut part A, the capsule, with a jigsaw, forming the bevel with a file. Drill both holes in part A using a spade bit and an electric drill. Part F, the hatch, should be cut from a piece of round molding with the table saw. Glue part E into part A, letting part E protrude 6 inches. Glue part F, the hatch, 2½ inches from the front of part A, with the edges of part F ⅛ inch from the bevel on part A.

PART F — 1⅜ ROUND MOLDING, ¼ LONG

PART E — ½ DOWEL, 7 LONG

Spacer, Pole, and
Washer
Parts B, C, and D

Use a hole saw and an electric drill to cut the spacer, part B. Drill the center with a spade bit and an electric drill. Cut part C, the pole, with a coping saw. Cut and drill part D, the washer, with a hole saw and an electric drill. Drill the center of part D, using a twist bit and an electric drill. Glue part C into part A, with tops flush. Slide part C through the spacer, part B, and the body, part K, and glue part C into part D, with bottoms flush. Part A should be firmly fitted to the body, part K, and turn freely.

2⅜ DIA. $\frac{3}{16}$ THICK

PART B

½ DRILL

PART C — ½ DOWEL, 3 LONG

PART D — 1⅜ ROUND MOLDING,
½ THICK, ½ DRILLED IN CENTER

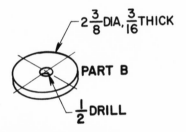

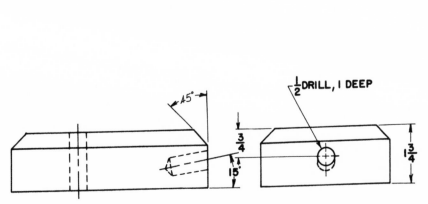

½ DRILL, 1 DEEP

45°

¾

15°

1¾

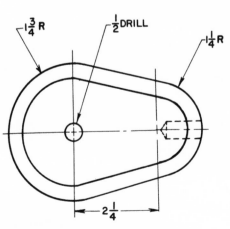

1¾ R

½ DRILL

1¼ R

2¼

PART A

Race Car

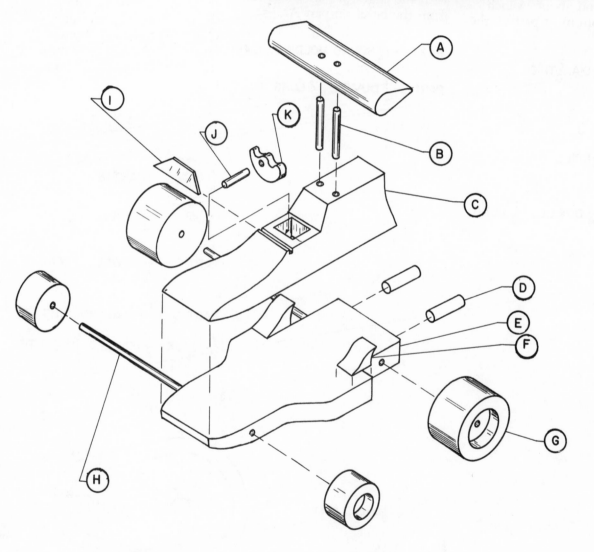

MATERIALS

LETTER	NUMBER REQUIRED	NAME	SIZE
A	1	AIR FOIL	4½ × 1¾ × ¾ inches
B	2	POST	¼-inch dowel, 2 inches long
C	1	UPPER BODY	10 × 3 × 1½ inches
D	2	TAIL PIPE	½-inch dowel, 1 inch long
E	1	BOTTOM BODY	10 × 5 × ¾ inches
F	2	FIN	1 × ½ × 1 inches
G	2	BACK WHEEL	2½ × 2½ × 1½ inches
—	2	FRONT WHEEL	2 × 2 × 1 inches
H	2	BACK AXLE	¼-inch dowel, 5 inches long
—	2	FRONT AXLE	¼-inch dowel, 4 inches long
I	1	WINDSHIELD	2 × ¾ × approximately ³⁄₃₂ inches, Plexiglas
J	1	STEERING SHAFT	¼-inch dowel, 1 inch long
K	1	STEERING WHEEL	1¼ × 1 × ¼ inches

TOOLS

Ruler
Hammer
Try square
Coping saw
Rasp
File
Table saw
Electric drill or drill press
Band saw
Belt sander
¼-inch twist bit
⁵⁄₁₆-inch twist bit
2½-inch hole saw
1¾-inch hole saw
1½-inch Forstner bit
⅞-inch Forstner bit

CONSTRUCTION NOTES

Body
Parts C, E, and F

Cut part C, the upper body, using a band saw. Using a coping saw, cut the square for the seat section. Drill a ¼-inch hole ½ inch deep for part J, the steering shaft, with an electric drill and a twist bit. Cut the saw kerf with a table saw. Also cut the bevel along the length of part C using a table saw. Drill the holes for part B, the post, using an electric drill and a twist bit.

Cut part E, the bottom body, using the band saw. Sand the contour shown in the side view of part E with a belt sander. Use a ⁵⁄₁₆-inch twist bit to drill the holes required for the axles. Glue part C, the upper body, to part E, the bottom body, keeping the front and rear portions flush. Drill two ½-inch holes, ¾ inch deep, in part E for the tail pipe, part D, using an electric drill and a twist bit. Cut part F, the fins, using a coping saw. Glue part F to part E as shown in the photograph.

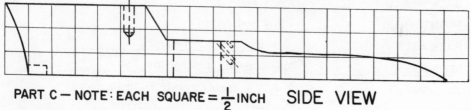

PART C — NOTE: EACH SQUARE = $\frac{1}{2}$ INCH   SIDE VIEW

PART F: NOTE: EACH SQUARE = $\frac{1}{4}$ INCH

LENGTH IS 1 INCH

TOP VIEW

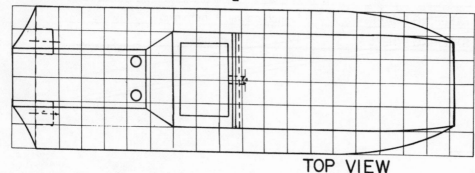

PART E — EACH SQUARE = $\frac{1}{2}$ INCH   SIDE VIEW

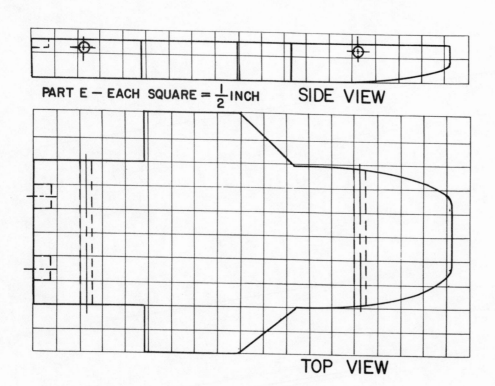

TOP VIEW

Air Foil
and Post
Parts A and B

Cut the air foil, part A, using a table saw, and file the contour as shown in the side view. Cut part B, the post, using a coping saw. Glue part B into part A, the air foil, with tops flush. Glue part B into part C, the upper body, leaving ⅝ inch between parts A and C.

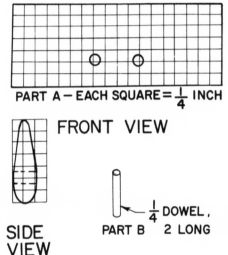

PART A — EACH SQUARE = ¼ INCH

FRONT VIEW

SIDE
VIEW

PART B ← ¼ DOWEL, 2 LONG

Steering Wheel
and Shaft and
Windshield
Parts I, J, and K

Using a band saw, cut a ¼-inch long piece of round molding. Cut the shape of the steering wheel, part K, using a coping saw. Drill the ¼-inch hole using an electric drill and a twist bit. Cut part J, the steering shaft, with a coping saw, and glue it into part K, the steering wheel, keeping the outside surfaces flush. Glue the protruding portion of part J into part C, the upper body, leaving ⅛ inch between parts C and K.

Using a coping saw, cut the windshield, part I. Carefully tap part I into the saw kerf of part C. A firm fit is required.

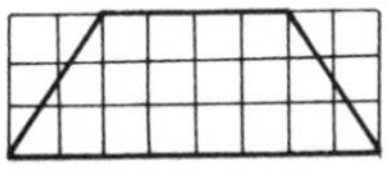

PART I — NOTE:
THICKNESS IS ⅛ INCH

← ¼ DOWEL, I LONG
PART J

PART K
NOTE: EACH SQUARE = ¼ INCH

THICKNESS IS ¼

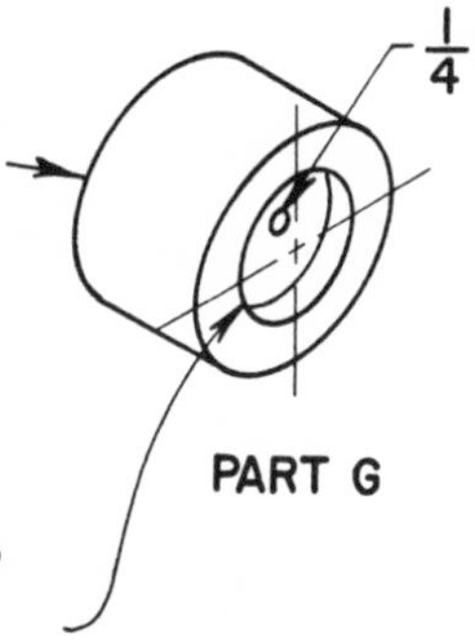

Tail Pipe
Part D

Cut part D, the tail pipe, using a coping saw. Drill a hole ½ inch deep in the end, using a twist bit and electric drill. Glue part D into the holes at the end of parts E and C, letting part D protrude ½ inch.

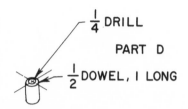

← ¼ DRILL

PART D

½ DOWEL, I LONG

Wheel
Parts G and H

Cut part G, the back and front wheels, using a hole saw and an electric drill. Drill the portion to be recessed, using a Forstner bit and an electric drill. Cut the axles, part H, to length with a coping saw. Slide the axle, part H, through the hole in part E. Glue the wheels, part G, to the axle, part H, with the outsides of the wheel and axle flush. Part H should rotate freely inside the holes in part E, the bottom body.

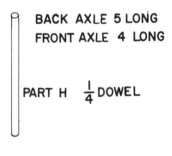

BACK AXLE 5 LONG
FRONT AXLE 4 LONG

PART H   ¼ DOWEL

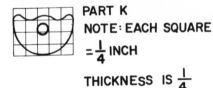

BACKWHEELS - 2½ DIA, 1½ THICK
FRONTWHEELS - 1¾ DIA, I THICK

← ¼ DRILL

PART G

BACKWHEELS - 1½ DRILL, ½ DEEP
FRONTWHEELS ⅞ DIA, ½ DEEP

Wrecker

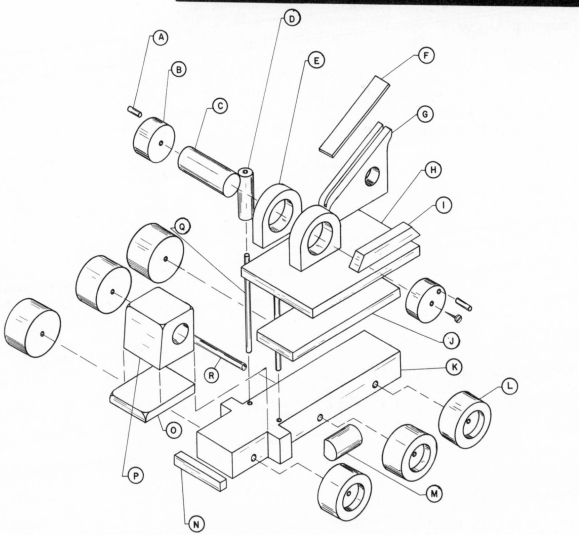

MATERIALS

LETTER	NUMBER REQUIRED	NAME	SIZE
A	2	CRANK HANDLE	¼-inch dowel, ¾ inches long
B	2	CRANK WHEEL	1½ × 1½ × ¾ inches
C	1	CRANK	1⅜-inch round molding, 3¼ inches long
D	2	MUFFLER	¾-inch dowel, 2 inches long
E	2	HOIST	2¾ × 2⅜ × ½ inches
F	1	STRING COVER	4¾ × ⅝ × ⅛ inches
G	1	BOOM	5 × 3½ × ¾ inches
H	1	BED	7⅞ × 5⅛ × ½ inches
I	2	RAIL	4¾ × ½ × ⅝ inches
J	1	SPACER	7⅝ × 2½ × ½ inches
K	1	FRAME	12 × 4⅛ × 1½ inches
L	6	WHEEL	2½ × 2½ × 1½ inches
M	2	GAS TANK	1⅜-inch round molding, 2¼ inches long
N	1	BUMPER	3½ × ½ × ½ inches
O	1	HOOD	3½ × 2½ × ½ inches
P	1	CAB	2½ × 2½ × 2½ inches
Q	2	EXHAUST PIPE	¼-inch dowel, 5⅝ inches long
R	3	AXLE	¼-inch dowel, 4¾ inches long

Thirty 1-inch wire brads
Ten No. 6 finishing nails

Four No. 4 finishing nails
Eight 1¼ × 10 flat head screws

Two 1¼ × 8 pan head screws

TOOLS

Wood file
Hammer
Nail set
Try square
Ruler
C-Clamp or hand screw clamp
Standard screwdriver
Coping saw

Jigsaw
Band saw
Table saw
Electric drill
2½-inch hole saw
1¾-inch hole saw
¾-inch spade bit
1⁷⁄₁₆-inch spade bit

1-inch spade bit
¼-inch twist bit
⅜-inch twist bit
1½-inch Forstner bit
Belt sander

CONSTRUCTION NOTES

Spacer, Frame, Hood, and Cab Parts J, K, O, and P

Cut the frame, part K, using a jigsaw. Drill the three holes required for the axle, part R, and the two 1-inch-deep holes for the exhaust pipe, part Q, with an electric drill and twist bit. Cut the spacer, part J, using a table saw. Glue and nail part J, the spacer, with four No. 4 finishing nails to the frame, part K, so that part J is flush with part K on the sides and back.

Cut the hood, part O, using a table saw. Round off the corners with a wood file as shown in the drawing. Use a table saw to cut the cab, part P. Drill the hole using a spade bit and an electric drill. Attach part P, the cab, and part O, the hood, flush on the back and sides, by gluing and clamping with a C-clamp. Attach parts P and O to the frame, part K, by gluing and clamping with a C-clamp, with the sides and fronts of parts K and O flush.

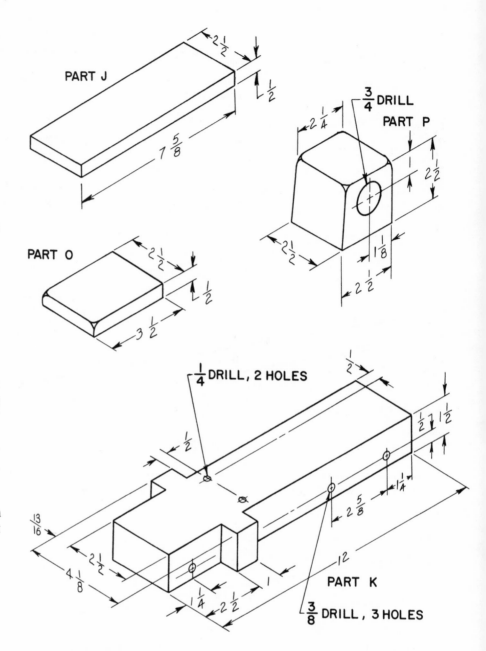

String Cover, Bed, Boom, and Rail Parts F, G, H, and I

Cut the bed, part H, with a table saw. Cut the rails, part I, on a jigsaw. The rails should fit flush with the bed sides and the back of the bed. Glue and nail the rails to the bed, using wire brads.

Before cutting part G, the boom, use a table saw to cut a saw kerf on a board that is at least 12 inches long. The extra-long board is used for safety. After the kerf has been cut use a jigsaw to cut the final shape. Drill the hole with a 1-inch spade bit and an electric drill. The boom should be centered from side to side on part H, the bed, flush in the back. Glue the boom to the bed and screw two flat head screws from the bottom of part H up into part G.

Cut part F, the string cover, using a table saw. Using two wire brads, but no glue, nail the string cover to the boom, part G, covering the saw kerf on the boom. Not using glue permits you to take the string cover off easily to replace the string when it becomes worn.

Do not attach the bed, part H, to the spacer, part J, until the cranking mechanism is finished and attached.

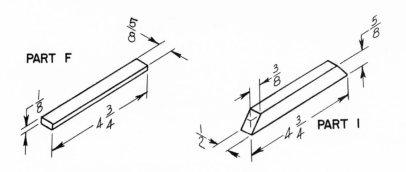

PART F

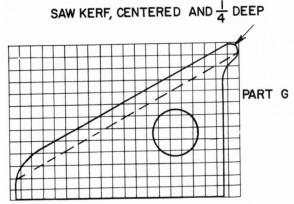

SAW KERF, CENTERED AND ¼ DEEP

PART I

PART G

NOTE: ¾ THICK, EACH SQUARE = ¼ INCH

Cranking Mechanism Parts A, B, C, and E

Cut the hoist, part E, on a jig-saw. Drill the holes with a spade bit and an electric drill. With glue and two flat head screws, attach part E, the hoist, to the bed, part H, so part E and part H are flush in front. Part E, the hoist, should be set in 1 inch from either side of the bed, part H.

Cut part C, the crank, using a table saw. Drill a hole ½ inch deep and the same diameter as the string selected for your truck. Make part B, the crank wheel, using a 1¾-inch hole saw and an electric drill. Drill the hole for part A, the crank handle, with a twist bit and an electric drill. Cut part A, the crank handle, and glue part A into part B, the crank wheel, so part A protrudes from part B ¼ inch on the out-side. Attach part C, the crank, and part B, the crank wheel, with pan head screws. Glue a string into the hole in part C, the crank, and slide the string through the saw kerf on part G, the boom. Cut the string to a length of 24 inches.

Attach the bed, part H, using glue and four No. 4 finishing nails, centering it on part J from side to side, with back surfaces flush.

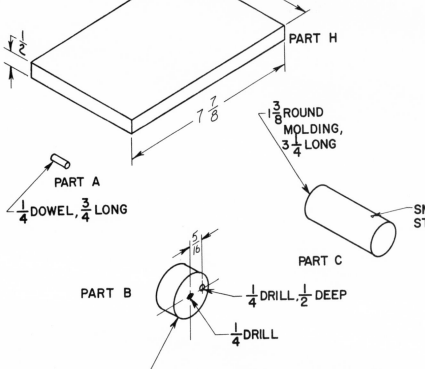

PART H

PART A
¼ DOWEL, ¾ LONG

1⅜ ROUND MOLDING, 3¼ LONG

PART C

SMALL HOLE TO ACCOM STRING

PART B
¼ DRILL, ½ DEEP
¼ DRILL
1½ DIA., ¾ THICK

1⅜ R
1⁷⁄₁₆ DRILL
PART E

82

Muffler and Exhaust Pipe Parts D and Q

Cut the dowel rods for part Q, the exhaust pipe, and part D, the muffler. Drill the hole through the muffler, part D, and glue part D onto the exhaust pipe, part Q, so the exhaust pipe protrudes above the muffler ½ inch. Glue part Q into part K so part Q extends 4⅝ inches above part K.

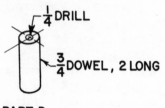

PART D

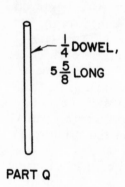

PART Q

Gas Tank and Bumper Parts M and N

Cut the gas tank, part M, from a piece of round molding, using a table saw. Flatten one side of the surface to ½ inch wide using a belt sander. Glue the flat surface of the gas tank to the frame, part K, and drive one No. 6 finishing nail through the gas tank. The gas tank, part M, should be centered vertically on the frame, part K, 5½ inches from the back of the frame. On the table saw cut part N, the bumper. Glue and nail it with wire brads to the frame, part K, ⅜ inch from the bottom and centered horizontally.

1⅜ ROUND MOLDING, 2¼ LONG

PART M

NOTE:
SLIGHTLY FLATTEN ON SIDE TO GLUE TO FRAME.

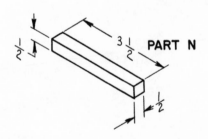

½ 3½ PART N ½

Wheel and Axle Parts L and R

Use a hole saw and an electric drill to cut the wheels, part L. Drill the centers out with a Forstner bit and an electric drill. Cut the dowel rod for the axles, part R, using a coping saw. Place the axles through the holes in the frame and glue the wheels to the axles.

2⅜ DIA., 1½ THICK

1½ DRILL, ½ DEEP

PART L — ¼ DRILL

NOTE: AXLE NOT SHOWN, 3 REQ'D ¼ DOWEL, 4 LONG

Jeep

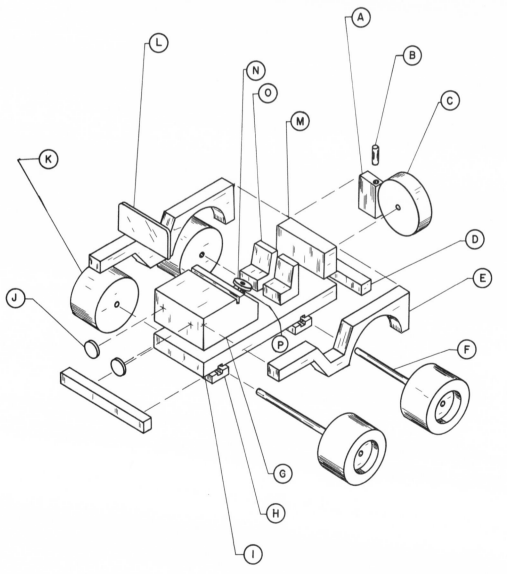

MATERIALS

LETTER	NUMBER REQUIRED	NAME	SIZE
A	1	GAS TANK	1¹¹⁄₁₆ × 1³⁄₁₆ × ½ inches
B	1	GAS CAP	¼-inch dowel, ¾ inch long
C	1	SPARE TIRE	2½ × 2½ × ¾ inches
D	2	BUMPER	4½ × ½ × ½ inches
E	2	FENDER	8 × 1⅞ × ¾ inches
F	2	AXLE	¼-inch dowel, 5¼ inches long
G	1	HOOD	3⅛ × 2⅞ × 1¾ inches
H	2	AXLE HOUSING	2⅞ × 1½ × ½ inches
I	1	BOTTOM	8 × 2⅞ × ¾ inches
J	2	HEADLIGHT	¾-inch dowel, ³⁄₁₆ inch long
K	4	WHEEL	2½ × 2½ × 1½ inches
L	1	WINDSHIELD	1½ × 2⅞ × approximately ⅛ inches, Plexiglas
M	1	REAR SUPPORT	1⅛ × 2⅞ × ¾ inches
N	1	STEERING WHEEL	1⅜-inch round molding, ¼ inch long
O	2	SEAT	1½ × 1¼ × 1 inches
P	1	STEERING COLUMN	¼-inch dowel, 1 inch long

Thirty 1-inch wire brads

TOOLS

Try square
Ruler
Hammer
Nail set
Coping saw
Table saw
½-inch electric drill
1½-inch Forstner bit
2½-inch hole saw
¼-inch twist bit

CONSTRUCTION NOTES

Frame
Parts G, I, and M

Cut part I, the bottom, on a table saw. Cut the grooves by making saw kerfs across the bottom, part I. Cut a groove ¼ inch deep on part G, the hood, for the windshield, part L, using the table saw. This should be done with a blade that cuts a kerf approximately the same width as the Plexiglas being used: some experimenting on a scrap piece of wood may be required to find the right blade. Cut the angle on part G, the hood. Using an electric drill and a ¼-inch twist bit, drill a hole into part G ¼ inch deep, ½ inch from the top, and ¾ inch from the left side: the steering column, part P, will fit here. Glue and nail with wire brads part G, the hood, to part I, the bottom, so the sides and fronts of the parts are flush. Cut part M on a table saw, and glue and nail it to part I, using wire brads. Part M should be flush with part I at the back and sides.

Fenders
Part E

Cut part E, the fenders, with a coping saw. Attach the fender to the frame using glue and wire brads. The fender should be flush with the frame both front and back. The top of the back portion of the fender should be flush with the top of part M, the rear support. The top of the front portion of the fender, part E, should be about ¼ inch below the top of the hood, part G. The bottom of the fender should be flush with the bottom of part I, the bottom.

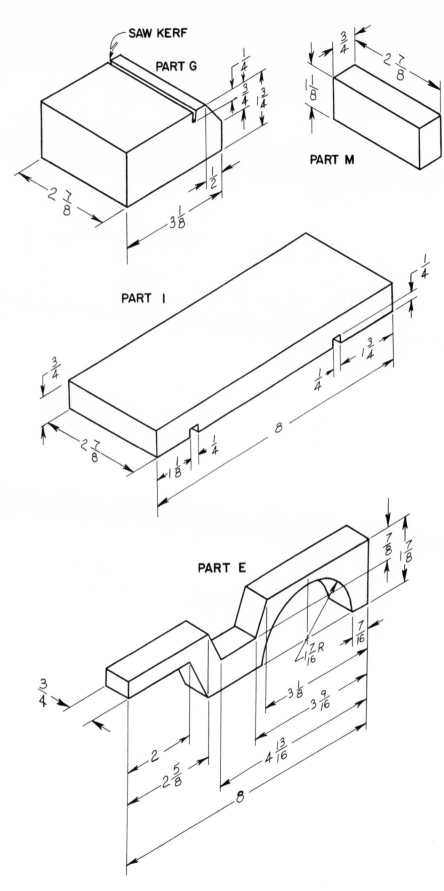

Axle Housing Part H

Cut two or three saw kerfs in a board at least 1 foot long to make the groove for part H, the axle housing. Then cut the shape for part H, the axle housing. Use of a board at least 1 foot long and use of a push stick will ensure a safe operation.

Glue and nail with wire brads part H to part I. Align the grooves on each part to form a large rectangular hole with sides flush.

Bumper and Headlight Parts D and J

Cut the bumper, part D, on a table saw. Glue and nail the bumper to the bottom, part I, so they are flush on the bottom and the bumper protrudes ¹³⁄₁₆ inch on the sides. Cut the headlights, part J, from a dowel rod; glue and nail part J to the hood of the jeep. The headlights should be ¼ inch in from the sides and ¼ inch down from the top of part G, the hood.

Gas Tank and Spare Tire Parts A, B, and C

Cut the gas tank, part A, on a table saw. Drill the hole for the gas cap, using an electric drill and a twist bit. Cut a dowel for the gas cap, part B, and glue part B into the hole in part A, letting it protrude ¼ inch. Glue and nail the gas tank, part A, onto the back of the jeep so part A rests on the bumper, part D, and is ½ inch in from the passenger side of the jeep.

Cut the spare tire, part C, using an electric drill and a hole saw. Drill part C using an electric drill and a Forstner bit. Attach part C to the rear of the jeep, centered between the driver's side edge of the jeep and the gas tank. Glue part C to the frame and nail with wire brads.

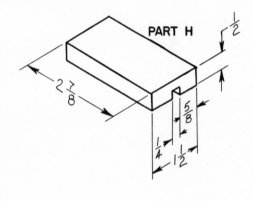

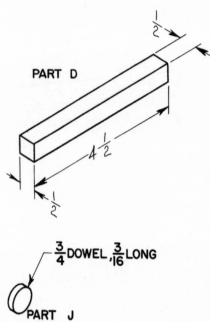

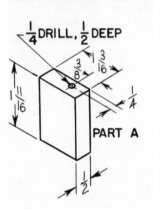

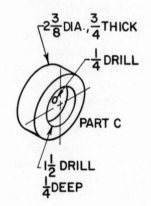

Steering Wheel and Seat Parts N, O, and P

The steering wheel, part N, may be cut on a table saw from a piece of round molding. Drill the center of part N, using an electric drill and a twist bit. Cut a ¼-inch dowel rod 1 inch long for the steering column, part P. Glue part P into the hood, part G. Part P should protrude from part G by ½ inch. Glue the steering wheel, part N, to part P, the steering column, with tops flush. Cut the seats, part O, with a coping saw. Glue and nail part O to the bottom, part I, leaving ½ to ⅝ inch of space between part O and part G, ¼ inch of space between the seats, and ¼ inch of space between the seats and the fender.

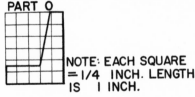

PART N

PART O

NOTE: EACH SQUARE = 1/4 INCH. LENGTH IS 1 INCH.

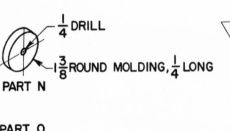

PART P

Wheel and Axle Parts F and K

Use a hole saw and an electric drill to cut the wheels, part K. Drill the centers out with an electric drill and a Forstner bit. Cut the dowels for the axles, part F. Slide the axle into the rectangular hole in parts H and I and glue the wheels, part K, to the axle flush outside. The axles should be free to turn in the rectangular holes.

$\frac{1}{4}$ DOWEL, $5\frac{1}{4}$ LONG

PART F

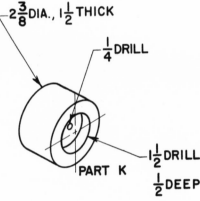

$2\frac{3}{8}$ DIA., $1\frac{1}{2}$ THICK

$\frac{1}{4}$ DRILL

PART K

$1\frac{1}{2}$ DRILL, $\frac{1}{2}$ DEEP

Windshield Part L

Cut the windshield, part L, out of Plexiglas, and sand the sides with a very fine wet-and-dry sandpaper. Very carefully tap the windshield into the saw kerf on part G, the hood. Placing a board under the jeep to raise the wheels off the ground provides a solid foundation to tap the windshield in place, instead of letting the jeep rest on the axle and tapping hard on the windshield, which could break the axles.

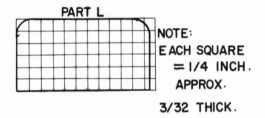

PART L

NOTE: EACH SQUARE = 1/4 INCH. APPROX.

3/32 THICK.

Semi-Tractor

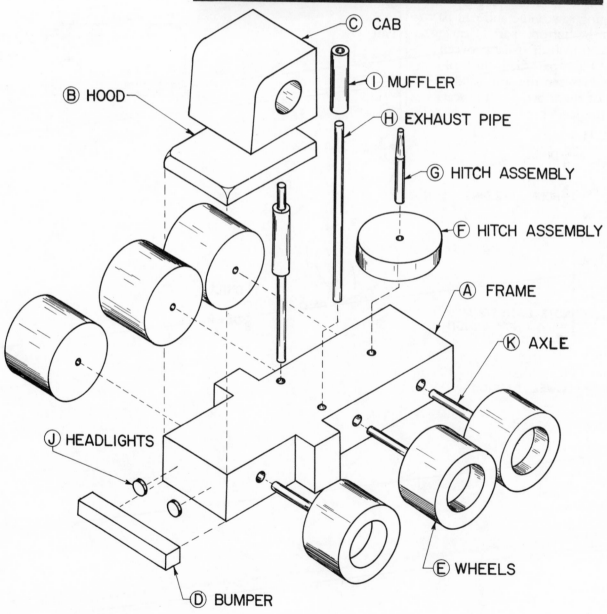

Ⓒ CAB

Ⓘ MUFFLER

Ⓑ HOOD

Ⓗ EXHAUST PIPE

Ⓖ HITCH ASSEMBLY

Ⓕ HITCH ASSEMBLY

Ⓐ FRAME

Ⓚ AXLE

Ⓙ HEADLIGHTS

Ⓔ WHEELS

Ⓓ BUMPER

MATERIALS

LETTER	NUMBER REQUIRED	NAME	SIZE
A	1	FRAME	8⁷⁄₁₆ × 4 × 1½ inches
B	1	HOOD	2½ × 3½ × ½ inches
C	1	CAB	2½ × 2⅝ × 2¼ inches
D	1	BUMPER	3½ × ½ × ½ inches
E	6	WHEEL	2½ × 2½ × 1½ inches
F	1	HITCH ASSEMBLY	2½ × 2½ × ½ inches
G	1	HITCH ASSEMBLY	¼-inch dowel, 2½ inches long
H	2	EXHAUST PIPE	¼-inch dowel, 6 inches long
I	2	MUFFLER	½-inch dowel, 2 inches long
J	2	HEADLIGHT	⅝ × ⅝ × ³⁄₁₆ inches
K	3	AXLE	¼-inch dowel, 6 inches long

Two No. 4 finishing nails

TOOLS

Coping saw
Wood file
Nail set
Claw hammer
C-clamps
Jigsaw or band saw
Table saw
Electric drill or drill press (½ inch)
Jointer
⅝-inch plug cutter
¼-inch twist bit
Spade bit
½-inch hole saw
1½-inch Forstner bit
Try square
Ruler

CONSTRUCTION NOTES

Frame, Hood, and Cab Parts A, B, and C

Cut the frame, part A, on a band saw. Drill the holes through the frame for the axle with an electric drill and twist bit. Then drill the two holes for the exhaust pipe, part E, and the hole for the hitch assembly, part G.

Cut the hood, part B, on a table saw and round the front top corner, as shown, using a wood file. Cut the cab, part C, on the table saw and drill the hole with a spade bit. Use two C-clamps when gluing parts A, B, and C together. Parts C and B should be flush on their backs and parts B and A should be flush in front.

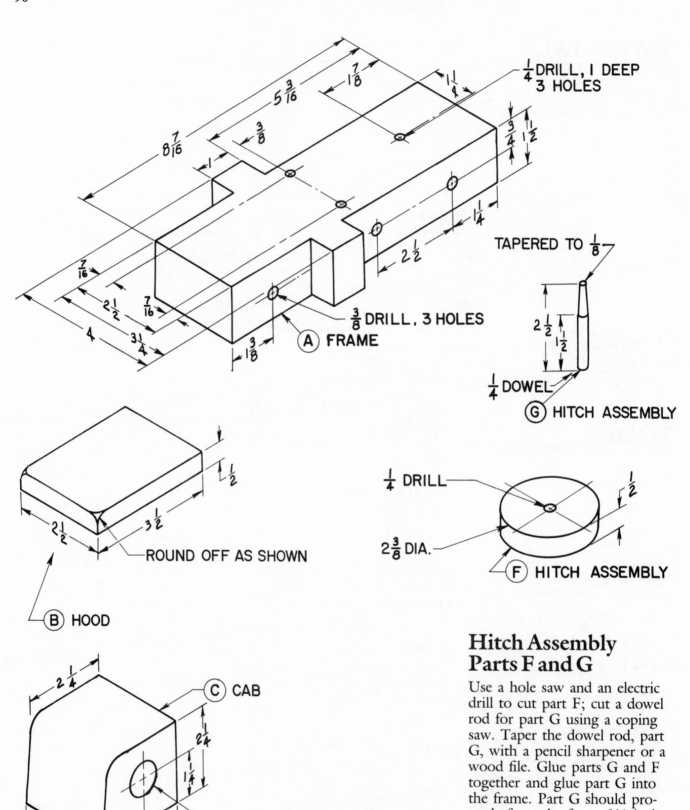

$5\frac{3}{16}$

$8\frac{7}{16}$

$1\frac{7}{8}$

$\frac{3}{8}$

1

$\frac{1}{4}$

$\frac{1}{4}$ DRILL, 1 DEEP
3 HOLES

$\frac{3}{4}$ $1\frac{1}{2}$

$\frac{7}{16}$

$2\frac{1}{2}$

$\frac{7}{16}$

4

$3\frac{1}{4}$

$1\frac{3}{8}$

$2\frac{1}{2}$

$1\frac{1}{4}$

$\frac{3}{8}$ DRILL, 3 HOLES

(A) FRAME

TAPERED TO $\frac{1}{8}$

$2\frac{1}{2}$

$1\frac{1}{2}$

$\frac{1}{4}$ DOWEL

(G) HITCH ASSEMBLY

$\frac{1}{2}$

$2\frac{1}{2}$ $3\frac{1}{2}$

ROUND OFF AS SHOWN

(B) HOOD

$\frac{1}{4}$ DRILL

$\frac{1}{2}$

$2\frac{3}{8}$ DIA.

(F) HITCH ASSEMBLY

$2\frac{1}{4}$

(C) CAB

$2\frac{1}{4}$

$1\frac{1}{4}$

$1\frac{1}{8}$

1 DRILL

$2\frac{1}{2}$

$2\frac{5}{8}$

Hitch Assembly
Parts F and G

Use a hole saw and an electric
drill to cut part F; cut a dowel
rod for part G using a coping
saw. Taper the dowel rod, part
G, with a pencil sharpener or a
wood file. Glue parts G and F
together and glue part G into
the frame. Part G should protrude from the frame 1½ inches.

Muffler and Exhaust Pipe Parts H and I

Cut the exhaust pipe, part H, and the muffler, part I, to length on a jigsaw. Drill the hole through part I, the muffler, using a twist bit and drill press. Glue the muffler, part I, onto the exhaust pipe, part H, so the top of the muffler is ½ inch below the top of the exhaust pipe. Then glue the exhaust pipe, part H, into the hole on the frame, part A, leaving 5 inches exposed.

Headlight and Bumper Parts J and D

Use a ⅝-inch plug cutter in an electric drill to cut the headlights, part J. Glue the headlights, part J, to the front of the truck so they are ½ inch from the top of part B and ¼ inch from the side. Cut the bumper, part D, on the table saw. Glue, nail with two No. 4 finishing nails, and attach it to the front of the frame, part A. Center it horizontally and place it ¼ inch above the bottom of the frame.

Wheel and Axle Parts E and K

Using an electric drill or drill press and a hole saw, cut the wheels, part E. Drill out their recessed centers with a Forstner bit. Cut the dowel rods for part K with a coping saw. Place the axles, part K, through the holes on the frame and glue the wheels, part E, onto the axles, with outsides flush.

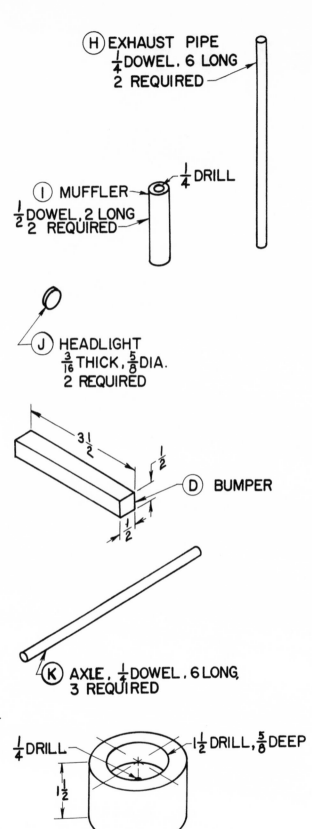

Flat-Bed Trailer

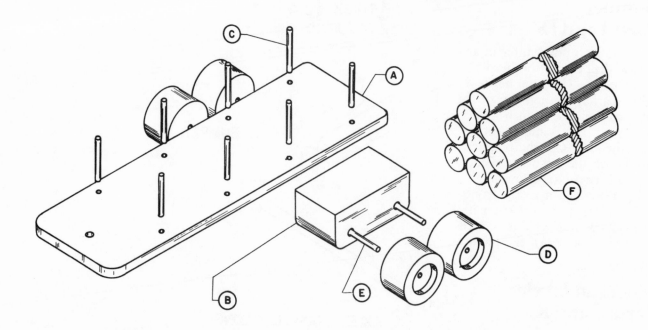

MATERIALS

LETTER	NUMBER REQUIRED	NAME	SIZE
A	1	BED	17¼ × 5¼ × ½ inches
B	1	AXLE HOUSING	4⅝ × 2⅝ × 2 inches
C	8	SIDE STAKE	¼-inch dowel, 2¾ inches long
D	4	WHEEL	2½ × 2½ × 1½ inches
E	2	AXLE	¼-inch dowel, 4⅝ inches long
F	9	LOG	1⅜-inch round molding, 13⅞ inches long

TOOLS

Hammer
Wood file
Coping saw
C-clamp
Try square
Ruler
Table saw
½-inch electric drill
Band saw (or use coping saw)
⅜-inch twist bit
¼-inch twist bit
2½-inch hole saw
1½-inch Forstner bit

CONSTRUCTION NOTES

Bed and Side Stakes Parts A and C

The bed, part A, should be cut on a table saw. Drill the holes for the side stakes, part C, using an electric drill and a twist bit. Round the corners slightly with a wood file. Drill the ⅜-inch hole with a twist bit and an electric drill. Cut the side stakes, part C, using a coping saw, and glue them into the holes so they are flush on the bottom with the bed, part A.

Axle Housing Part B

The axle housing, part B, should be cut out on the table saw. Round the corners with a band saw, coping saw, or file. Drill the two holes for the axle, part E. The axle housing, part B, should be placed 1 inch from the back of the bed and centered from side to side. Glue the axle housing, part B, to the bed, part A, using a C-clamp to secure it.

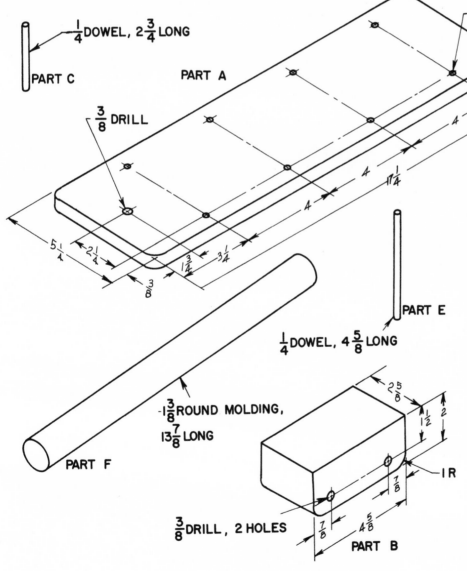

Wheel and Axle Parts D and E

Cut the wheels, part D, using an electric drill and a hole saw. Drill the centers out with a Forstner bit. Cut the dowel rods for the axles, part E, using a coping saw. Slide the axle through the holes in the axle housing, part B, and glue the wheels onto the axle.

Log Part F

You may either use round molding or turn the logs on a wood lathe. In either case, cut them to length with a table saw. Lay the logs on the bed as shown.

Enclosed Trailer

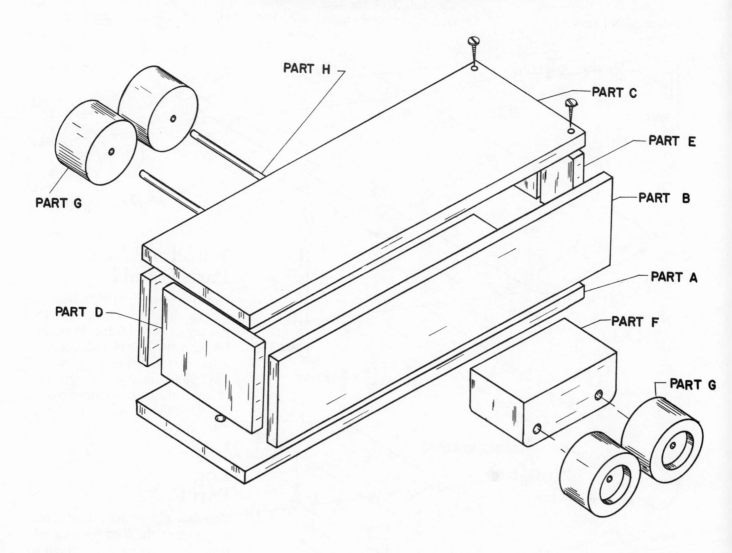

PART H

PART C

PART E

PART G

PART B

PART A

PART D

PART F

PART G

MATERIALS

LETTER	NUMBER REQUIRED	NAME	SIZE
A	1	BED	16¾ × 5⅜ × ½ inches
B	2	SIDE	16¾ × 3⅜ × ½ inches
C	1	TOP	16¾ × 5⅜ × ½ inches
D	1	FRONT END	4⅜ × 3⅜ × ½ inches
E	2	DOORS	3⁵⁄₁₆ × 2⅛ × ½ inches
F	1	AXLE HOUSING	4⅝ × 2 × 2⅝ inches
G	4	WHEEL	2½ × 2½ × 1½ inches
H	2	AXLE	¼-inch dowel, 4⅝ inches long

Thirty No. 4 finishing nails
Four 1 × 10 round head wood screws

TOOLS

Claw hammer
Nail set
Table saw
Try square
Ruler
Coping saw
Wood file

½-inch electric drill
1½-inch Forstner bit
2½-inch hole saw
¼-inch twist bit
⅜-inch twist bit
Standard screwdriver

CONSTRUCTION NOTES

Trailer Parts A, B, C, D, and E

Resaw, on the table saw, enough lumber to a thickness of ½ inch to make parts A, B, C, D, and E, then use the table saw to cut the parts. Drill the hole in part A, the bed, using a twist bit and an electric drill. Attach part B, the sides, to part A, the bed, and part C, the top, with all edges flush. Glue and nail parts A, B, and C, using finishing nails.

After these parts have been joined, part D, the front end, should fit snugly in the end of the trailer. Glue and nail part D, the front end, using finishing nails equally spaced on each side, top, and bottom. The outside of part D should be flush with the ends of parts A, B, and C. Drill the two holes into part A, the bed, and part C, the top, in which the doors, part E, will pivot. Place the doors, part E, in the back of the trailer and screw the round headed wood screws into the doors. Tighten the screws so the doors will open and close firmly.

Axle Housing Part F

Cut the axle housing, part F, on a table saw, then file the corners round with a wood file. Drill the two holes for the axle, part H, with a twist bit and an electric drill. Glue the axle housing, part F, on the bottom of part A, the bed, using a hand screw clamp to secure it until the glue dries. The axle housing should be centered from side to side and 2¼ inches from the back end.

96

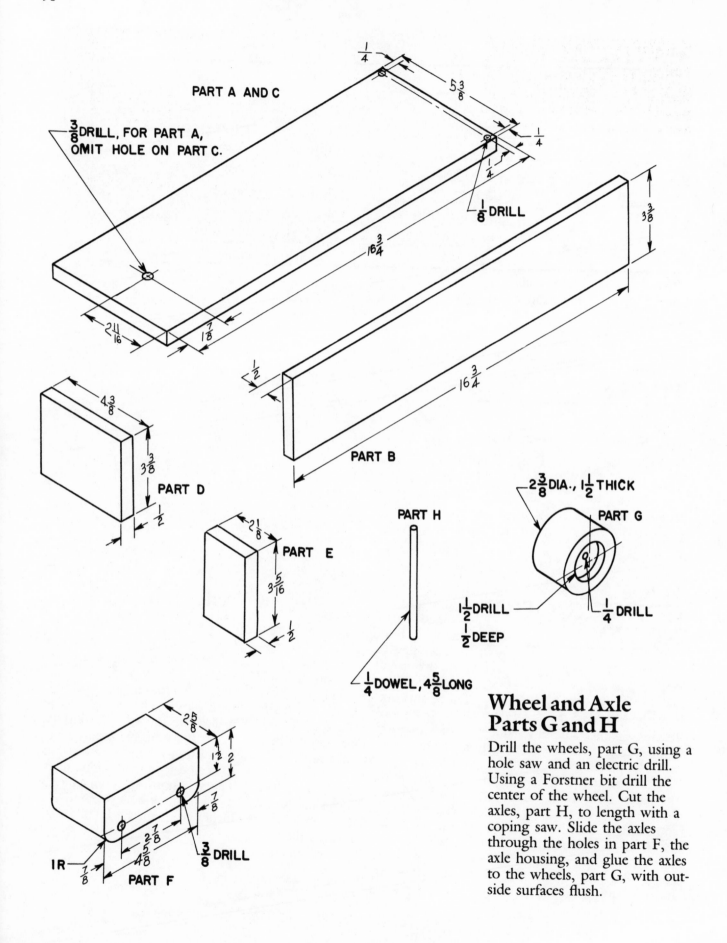

PART A AND C

3/8 DRILL, FOR PART A,
OMIT HOLE ON PART C.

1/4

5 3/8

1/4

1/4

1/8 DRILL

3 3/8

16 3/4

2 11/16

1 7/8

4 3/8

3 3/8

1/2

PART D

1/2

16 3/4

PART B

PART E

2 1/8

3 5/16

1/2

PART H

1/4 DOWEL, 4 5/8 LONG

2 3/8 DIA., 1 1/2 THICK

PART G

1 1/2 DRILL
1/2 DEEP

1/4 DRILL

Wheel and Axle
Parts G and H

Drill the wheels, part G, using a hole saw and an electric drill. Using a Forstner bit drill the center of the wheel. Cut the axles, part H, to length with a coping saw. Slide the axles through the holes in part F, the axle housing, and glue the axles to the wheels, part G, with outside surfaces flush.

2 5/8

2

1 1/2

7/8

2 7/8

2 5/8

4 5/8

3/8 DRILL

1 R

1/8

PART F

Tanker Trailer

MATERIALS

LETTER	NUMBER REQUIRED	NAME	SIZE
A	1	BED	15 × 4 × ½ inches
B	1	TANK	4⅝ × 4⅝ × 15 inches
C	2	TANK SUPPORT	5 × 1⅝ × ¾ inches
D	1	AXLE HOUSING	4⅝ × 2⅝ × 2 inches
E	2	AXLE	¼-inch dowel, 4⅝ inches long
F	4	WHEEL	2½ × 2½ × 1½ inches

Two No. 10 × 2 flat head screws

TOOLS

Try square
Ruler
Wood file
Clamps
Nail set
Claw hammer
Coping saw
Standard screwdriver
Table saw
Wood lathe
Electric drill
⅜-inch twist bit
2½-inch hole saw
1½-inch Forstner bit

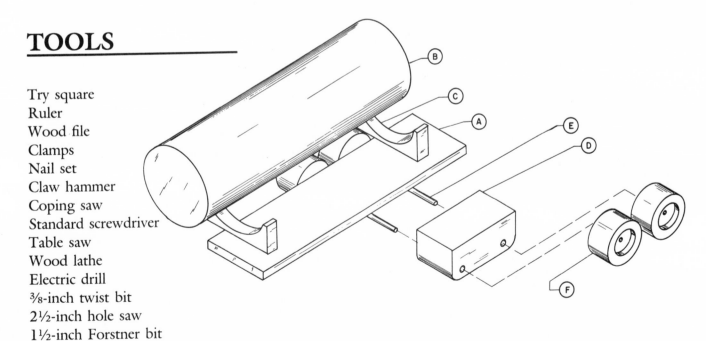

CONSTRUCTION NOTES

Bed and Tank Support Parts A and C

Cut part A, the bed, on the table saw. Drill the hole to accept the hitch from the semi-tractor with a twist bit and an electric drill. Cut part C, the tank support, with a coping saw. Glue part C to part A so the sides are flush, and the tank supports are 2¼ inches from the ends of the bed.

Tank Part B

Turn the tank, part B, to the correct size on a wood lathe. Sand it completely while on the lathe. Place part B on the tank supports, part C, and use two No. 10 by 2 flat head wood screws to attach part B from the bottom of the bed, part A. The tank, part B, should be even with each end of the bed, part A. The wood screws should be placed so they will go through the bed, part A, through the center of the tank supports, part C, and into the tank, part B.

Axle Housing Part D

Cut the axle housing, part D, using a table saw, and round the corners with a wood file. Drill the holes using a twist bit and an electric drill. Glue and clamp part D to the bed, part A, so it is 1½ inches from the back of the bed, centered on part A from side to side.

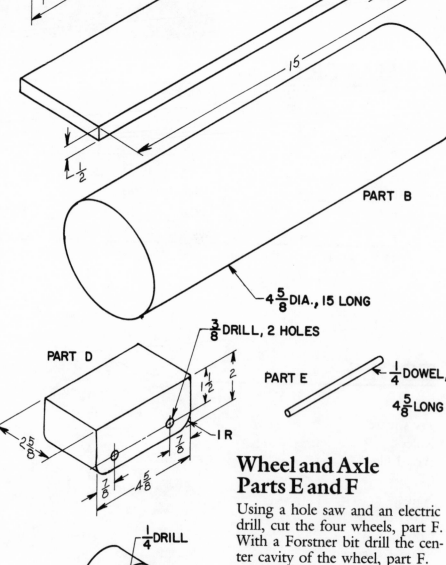

Wheel and Axle Parts E and F

Using a hole saw and an electric drill, cut the four wheels, part F. With a Forstner bit drill the center cavity of the wheel, part F. Cut the axle, part E, from a dowel rod using a coping saw. Slide the axles through the holes in the axle housing, part D, and glue the wheels, part F, on the axles, part E, with outside surfaces flush.

Auto Carrier
Trailer

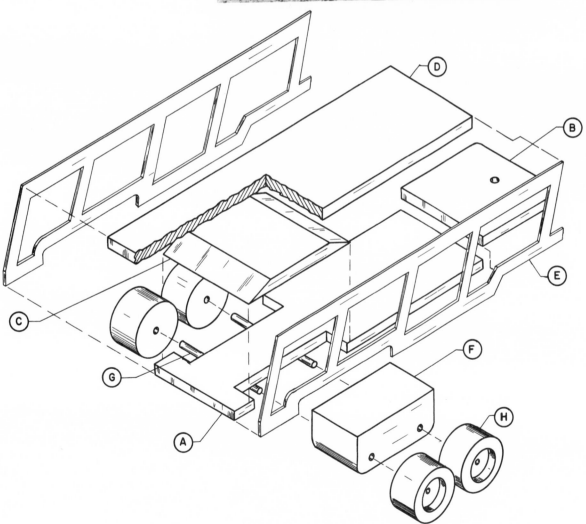

MATERIALS

LETTER	NUMBER REQUIRED	NAME	SIZE
A	1	BACK LOWER BED	13⅞ × 5 × ½ inches
B	1	FRONT LOWER BED	4½ × 5 × ½ inches
C	1	WHEEL COVER	6 × 5 × ½ inches
D	1	UPPER BED	16¹¹⁄₁₆ × 5 × ½ inches
E	2	SIDE	18 × 5 × ¼ inches
F	1	REAR END	4⅝ × 2⅝ × 2 inches
G	2	AXLE	¼-inch dowel, 4⅝ inches long
H	4	WHEEL	2⅜ × 1½ inches

Thirty 1-inch wire brads

TOOLS

Hammer
Nail set
Wood file
Try square
Ruler
Coping saw
Table saw
½-inch electric drill
2½-inch hole saw
1½-inch Forstner bit
⅜-inch twist bit or spade bit

CONSTRUCTION NOTES

Bed
Parts A, B, C, D, and E

Using a table saw, resaw enough lumber to a thickness of ½ inch to make parts A, B, C, and D and cut the parts on the table saw. Cut the notch in part A, the back lower bed, using a coping saw; also cut the rounded corners on part B, the front lower bed, with a coping saw. Drill the hole in part B, the lower bed, with an electric drill and a twist bit or spade bit. Cut the angles on part C, the wheel cover, using a table saw, or file them with a wood file. Cut the side, part E, with a coping saw. Glue part E, the sides, to part A, the back lower bed, and nail with wire brads. Part A should be flush with part E on bottom and back.

Nail with 1-inch wire brads part B, the front lower bed, so it is flush with the bottom of the front section of part E, the sides, and protrudes 1¼ inches in front.

Glue and clamp part C, the wheel cover, onto part A, the back lower bed. Part C should be the same width as part A and should overlap the notch on part A by ¼ inch on each end. Glue and nail with 1-inch wire brads part D, the upper bed, to part E, the sides, so that part D is ⅛ inch below the top of part E, with both parts flush in front.

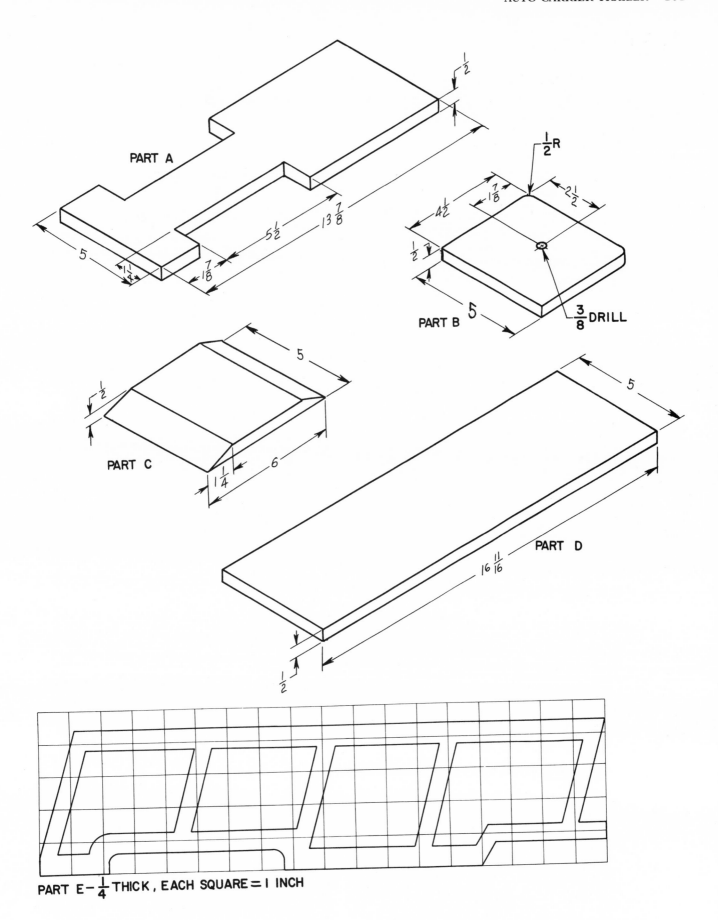

PART A

PART B

PART C

PART D

PART E—¼ THICK, EACH SQUARE = 1 INCH

Rear End
Part F

Cut the rear end, part F, with a table saw and round it with a wood file. Drill the two holes, using a twist bit and an electric drill. Center the rear end, part F, from side to side on the underside of part A, the back lower bed, 2⅝ inches from the back of part A. Glue part F to part A, securing it with a hand screw clamp until the glue dries.

Wheel and Axle
Parts G and H

Use a hole saw and an electric drill to cut the wheel, part H. Drill the centers with a Forstner bit. Cut the axles, part G, to length with a coping saw. Slide the axle, part G, through the rear end, part F, and glue the wheel, part H, to the axle so the axle is flush with the outside of the wheel on both sides.

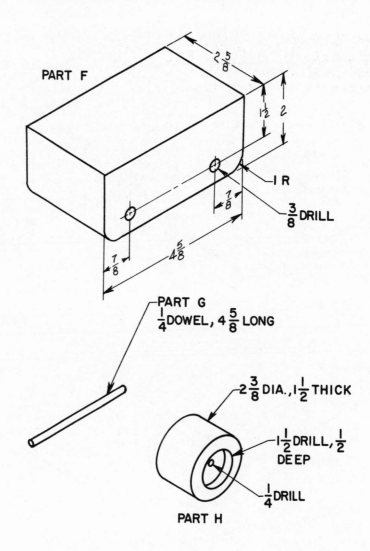

PART F

PART G
¼ DOWEL, 4⅝ LONG

2⅜ DIA., 1½ THICK

1½ DRILL, ½ DEEP

¼ DRILL

PART H

Tractor

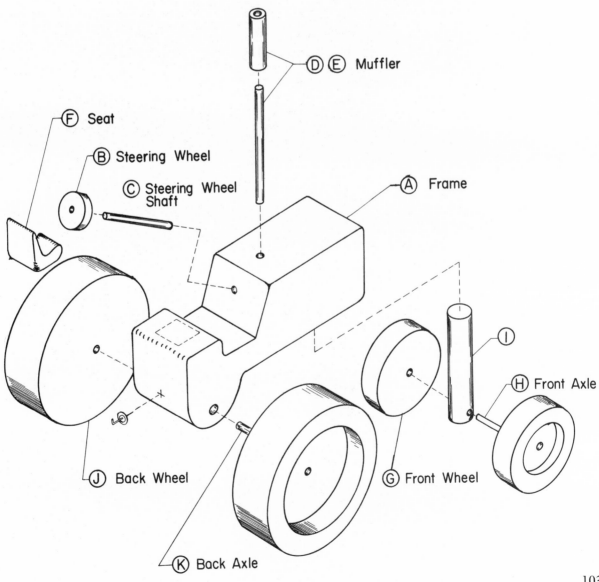

(D)(E) Muffler

(F) Seat

(B) Steering Wheel

(C) Steering Wheel Shaft

(A) Frame

(I)

(H) Front Axle

(J) Back Wheel

(G) Front Wheel

(K) Back Axle

MATERIALS

LETTER	NUMBER REQUIRED	NAME	SIZE
A	1	FRAME	7⅝ × 2¼ × 3⅝ inches
B	1	STEERING WHEEL	1¼-inch dowel, ⅜ inches long
C	1	STEERING WHEEL SHAFT	¼-inch dowel, 2½ inches long
D	1	MUFFLER	½-inch dowel, 2¼ inches long
E	1	MUFFLER EXHAUST PIPE	¼-inch dowel, 4¼ inches long
F	1	SEAT	1½ × 1¼ × 1⅜ inches
G	2	FRONT WHEEL	2½ × 2½ × ¾ inches
H	1	FRONT AXLE	¼-inch dowel, 1¾ inches long
I	1	FRONT AXLE HOUSING	¾-inch dowel, 1¾ inches long
J	2	BACK WHEEL	4⅝ × 4⅝ × 1½ inches long
K	1	BACK AXLE	¼-inch dowel, 4½ inches long

One No. 4 finishing nail

TOOLS

C-clamps
Jack plane
Hammer
Try square
Ruler
Compass
Band saw
Electric drill or drill press (½ inch)
Lathe
Lathe tools
Jointer
¾-inch spade bit
2½-inch hole saw
1½-inch Forstner bit
¼-inch twist bit
⅜-inch twist bit
⁵⁄₁₆-inch twist bit

CONSTRUCTION NOTES

Frame
Part A

Glue two pieces of 2-by-6 lumber long enough to make part A. Using a jointer or hand plane, plane the stock to its correct thickness, and use a band saw to cut the shape. Drill the hole for part I, using an electric drill and a space bit. Drill the holes for parts C, E, and K with a twist bit, drilling through the stock for part K.

Muffler and Exhaust Pipe
Parts D and E

Cut part E, the exhaust pipe, and part D, the muffler, to length using the band saw. Drill the hole in part D with a twist bit and an electric drill. Slide part D onto part E and glue it, leaving the exhaust pipe protruding from the muffler ⅜ inch. Glue the exhaust pipe into part A, the frame, letting it protrude 3¼ inches.

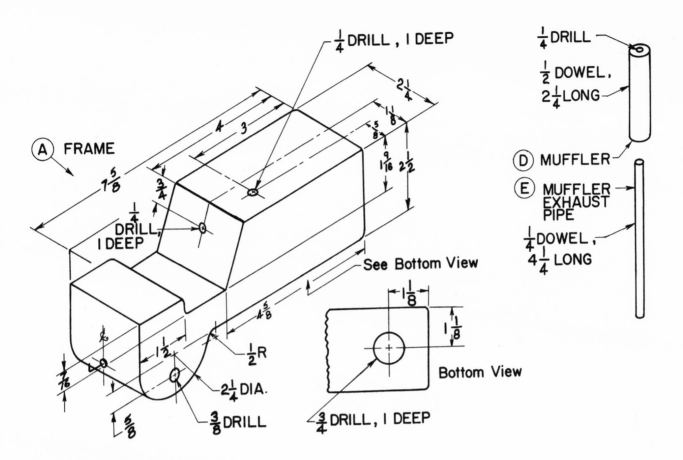

$\frac{1}{4}$ DRILL, I DEEP

Ⓐ FRAME

$1\frac{5}{8}$

DRILL, I DEEP
$\frac{1}{4}$

$\frac{3}{4}$

4
3

$2\frac{1}{4}$

$1\frac{1}{8}$

$\frac{5}{8}$

$\frac{9}{16}$ $2\frac{1}{2}$

See Bottom View

$4\frac{5}{8}$

$\frac{1}{2}$R

$1\frac{1}{2}$

$2\frac{1}{4}$ DIA.

$\frac{3}{8}$ DRILL

$\frac{7}{16}$

$\frac{5}{8}$

$\frac{1}{4}$ DRILL

$\frac{1}{2}$ DOWEL,
$2\frac{1}{4}$ LONG

Ⓓ MUFFLER

Ⓔ MUFFLER
EXHAUST
PIPE

$\frac{1}{4}$ DOWEL,
$4\frac{1}{4}$ LONG

$1\frac{1}{8}$

$1\frac{1}{8}$

Bottom View

$\frac{3}{4}$ DRILL, I DEEP

Seat and Steering Wheel
Parts B, C, and F

Cut the dowel rod for the steering wheel shaft, part C, and the round molding for the steering wheel, part B, using a band saw. Drill the hole in the steering wheel with a twist bit and an electric drill. Glue the steering shaft, part C, into the frame, part A. Part C should protrude 1¼ inches. Glue the steering wheel, part B, to the steering wheel shaft, part C, so they are flush on top.

Cut the seat, part F, on the band saw. Glue and nail it to the frame in the approximate area shown on the exploded view.

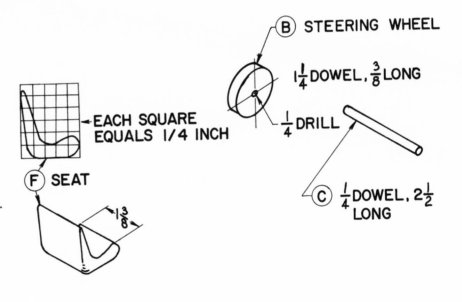

←EACH SQUARE
EQUALS 1/4 INCH

Ⓕ SEAT

$\frac{3}{8}$

Ⓑ STEERING WHEEL

$1\frac{1}{4}$ DOWEL, $\frac{3}{8}$ LONG

$\frac{1}{4}$ DRILL

Ⓒ $\frac{1}{4}$ DOWEL, $2\frac{1}{2}$
LONG

Front Wheel
Parts G, H, and I

Cut part I, the front axle housing, using a band saw. Drill with a twist bit a 5/16-inch hole through part I, for the front axle to rotate inside. Next glue part I into the frame, with 2¼ inches protruding. Cut the dowel for the front axle, part H, using a coping saw. Use a hole saw in an electric drill or drill press to cut the front wheels, part G. Drill the recessed part of the front wheels using a Forstner bit. Slide the axle through the hole in part I and glue the wheels, part G, to the axle, part H, so part G is flush outside with the ends of the axle, part H.

Back Wheel
Parts J and K

Using a wood lathe, turn the back wheels, part J. Cut the axle, part K, to the correct length with a band saw. Slide the axle, part K, through the hole in the frame, part A, and glue the back wheels, part J, to the axle, with outside surfaces flush.

Note: If the tractor is used to pull a disk, farm trailer, or plow, buy a small L-shaped hook and screw it in the back: 1½ inches down from the seat and centered.

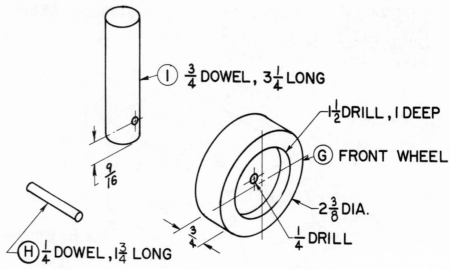

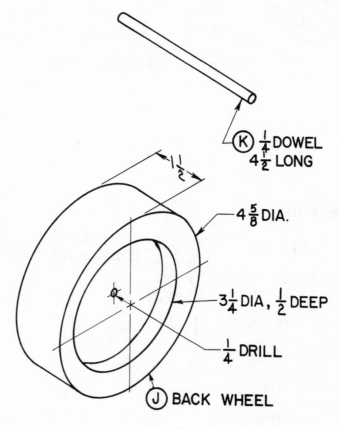

Farm Trailer

MATERIALS

LETTER	NUMBER REQUIRED	NAME	SIZE
A	1	BED	6¹⁄₁₆ × 14³⁄₈ × ½ inches
B	4	WHEEL	2³⁄₈ inches in diameter × ¾ inch thick
C	2	AXLE	¼-inch dowel, 7¼ inches long
D	2	AXLE HOUSING	6¹⁄₁₆ × 2³⁄₈ × 1½ inches
E	1	TONGUE	5¼ × ½ × ³⁄₁₆ inches

One No. 8 × ⅝ inches round
head wood screw

TOOLS

Clamps
Standard screwdriver
Try square
Ruler
Hammer
Table saw
½-inch electric drill
2½-inch hole saw
1½-inch Forstner bit
¼-inch twist bit
⅜-inch twist bit
³⁄₁₆-inch twist bit

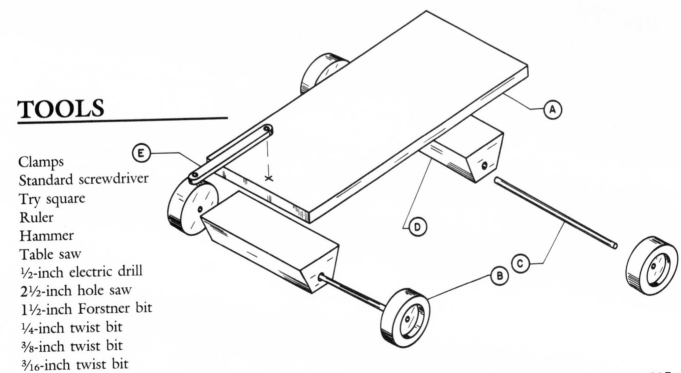

CONSTRUCTION NOTES

Bed and Tongue Parts A and E

Cut part A, the bed, and part E, the tongue, on the table saw. Drill the two holes in part E with a twist bit and an electric drill. Attach the tongue to the bed, using a round head screw. Part E should be centered on part A from side to side, and ½ inch back from the front.

Axle Housing Part D

Cut the axle housing, part D, on a table saw, drilling the holes with a twist bit. Glue the axle housing, part D, to the bottom of the bed, part A, and secure it with C-clamps or hand screw clamps until the glue dries.

Wheel and Axle Parts B and C

Cut the dowel rod for the axles, part C, with the table saw. Cut the wheel, part B, with a hole saw and an electric drill. Slide the axle, part C, through the axle housing, part D, and glue on the wheels, part B, with the outsides of part C and part B flush.

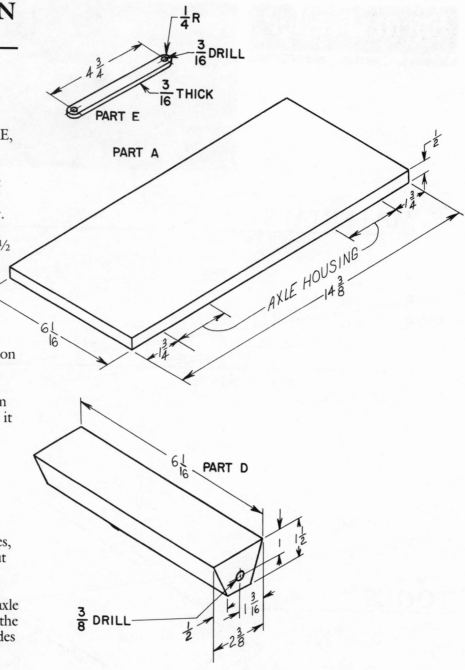

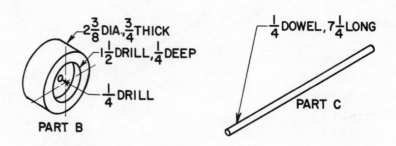

Disk

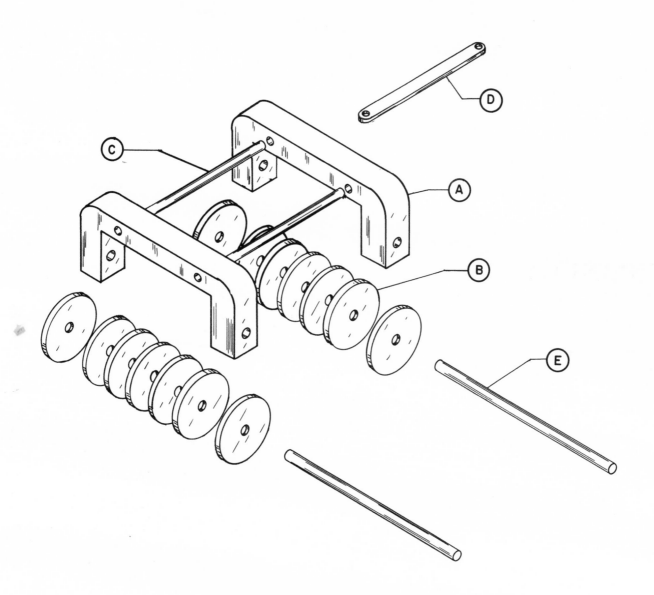

MATERIALS

LETTER	NUMBER REQUIRED	NAME	SIZE
A	2	FRAME	5⅛ × 2 × ¾ inches
B	14	DISK	1¾-inch diameter, 3/16 inch long
C	2	BRACE	¼-inch dowel, 4 7/16 inches long
D	1	TONGUE	4½ × ¾ × ¼ inches
E	2	AXLE	¼-inch dowel × 5⅞ inches

One No. 8 × ¾ round head
   wood screw

TOOLS

Try square
Ruler
Coping saw
Electric drill
Table saw
¼-inch twist bit
5/16-inch twist bit
1/16-inch twist bit
2-inch hole saw

CONSTRUCTION NOTES

Frame Parts A and C

The frame, part A, should be made from a wood that will ensure more strength than white pine: preferably a hardwood such as maple, cherry, or oak. Cut part A with a coping saw. Drill the holes required with a twist bit and an electric drill. Using a coping saw cut the dowel rod for part C, the braces. Glue part C, the braces, into part A, the frame, with outside surfaces flush. The two pieces for part A should be 2¹⁵/₁₆ inches apart and parallel.

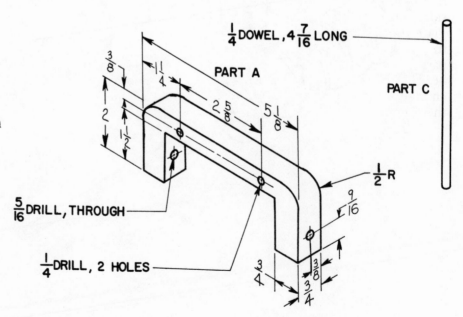

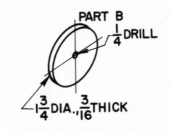

PART B
$\frac{1}{4}$ DRILL

$1\frac{3}{4}$ DIA., $\frac{3}{16}$ THICK

Disk and Axle
Parts B and E

Resaw a piece of lumber on the table saw large enough to make the 14 disks. With an electric drill and hole saw cut out the disk, part B. Cut part E, the axle, to its required length. Place a drop or two of glue inside each hole in each disk. Slide the axle, part E, through one hole in the frame, part A, then through five disks, part B. Continue sliding the axle, part E, through the other hole on the frame and place a disk on the outside of each side of the frame, part A, flush with the end of the axle. Space the five disks equally inside the frame, part A. The axle, part E, should turn smoothly inside the holes in part A.

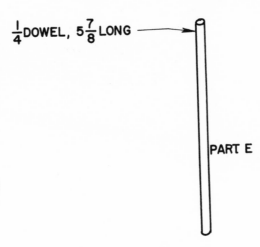

$\frac{1}{4}$ DOWEL, $5\frac{7}{8}$ LONG

PART E

Tongue
Part D

Cut the tongue, part D, using a coping saw. Drill the two holes with a twist bit and an electric drill. Drill a $\frac{1}{16}$-inch hole in the top of the front piece of part A, the frame, centered from side to side and from front to back. Place the end of the tongue over the $\frac{1}{16}$-inch hole in the top of part A and screw in the round head screw. Leave it loose enough for easy movement of the tongue.

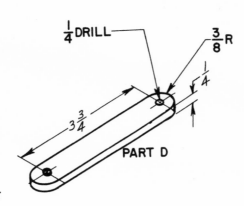

$\frac{1}{4}$ DRILL

$\frac{3}{8}$ R

$\frac{1}{4}$

$3\frac{3}{4}$

PART D

Plow

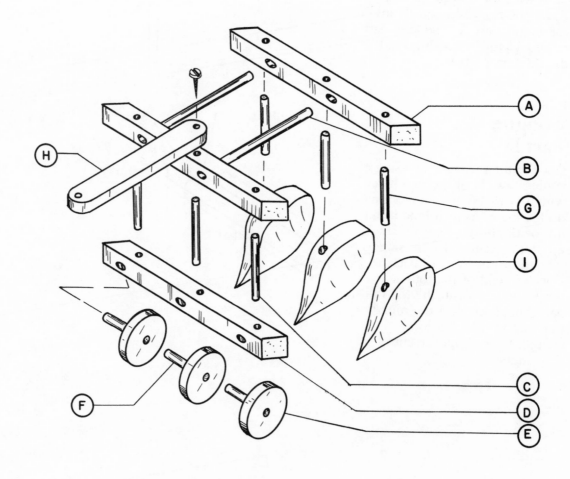

MATERIALS

LETTER	NUMBER REQUIRED	NAME	SIZE
A	2	FRAME BRACKET	5¾ × ½ × ½ inches
B	2	FRAME ROD	¼-inch dowel, 4 inches long
C	3	SUPPORT BAR ROD	¼-inch dowel, 1¾ inches long
D	1	DISK SUPPORT BAR	5¾ × ½ × ½ inches
E	3	DISK	1½ inches in diameter × ¼ inch thick
F	3	DISK ROD	¼-inch dowel, 1½ inches long
G	3	PLOW ROD	¼-inch dowel, 1½ inches long
H	1	TONGUE	4½ × ½ × ³⁄₁₆ inches
I	3	PLOW	2⅞ × 1½ × 1⁵⁄₁₆ inches

One No. 8 × ⅝ round head
screw

TOOLS

Try square
Ruler
Coping saw
Standard screwdriver
Table saw
¼-inch electric drill
¼-inch twist bit
¹⁄₁₆-inch twist bit
³⁄₁₆-inch twist bit
1½-inch hole saw

CONSTRUCTION NOTES

Frame
Parts A and B

Cut part A, using a table saw. Drill the holes with a twist bit and an electric drill for part G, part C, and part B. Using the table saw cut the dowel rods for part B. Glue these into part A so they are flush on the outside. The two pieces used for part A should be 3 inches apart and parallel.

Plow
Parts G and I

You can cut a cove in a board on the table saw to create the curved part of the plow (see Cutting Coves in the chapter titled Helpful Hints). Or you can make the cove by hand filing with a wood file or sanding with a drum sander. Cut the plows with a coping saw, and drill the holes with a twist bit and an electric drill. Cut the dowels for part G with a coping saw. Glue part G into part A, flush on top. Then glue on the plows, part I.

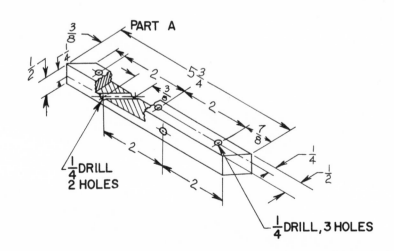

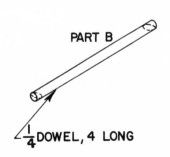

Disk and Support Bar and Rod Parts C, D, E, and F

Using a coping saw cut the dowel rods for part C. Cut part D, the disk support bar, on the table saw and drill the holes with a twist bit and an electric drill. Cut part F using a coping saw. The disk, part E, can be made using a hole saw. Glue part C into part A, flush on top. Then glue the disk, part E, to part F so part F is flush outside with part E. Glue part F into part D. Once parts E, F, and D are glued together as one unit, glue part C to part D. This may require some adjustment up or down to keep the plow level. Once adjusted, glue parts D and C.

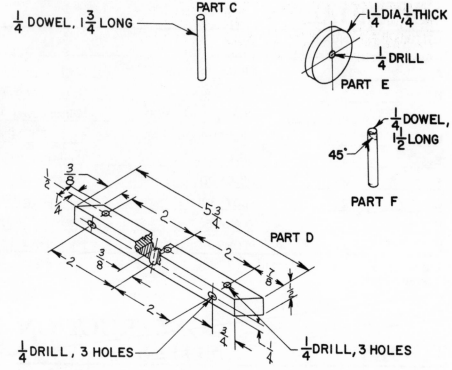

Tongue Part H

Cut the tongue, part H, on the table saw, rounding the ends with a coping saw. Drill the holes with a twist bit and an electric drill. Drill a 1/16-inch hole into the center dowel rod from the top of part A. Put the round head wood screw through either hole on part H and drive it into the 1/16-inch hole drilled in the dowel in part A. Tighten the screw but allow for movement of the tongue, part H.

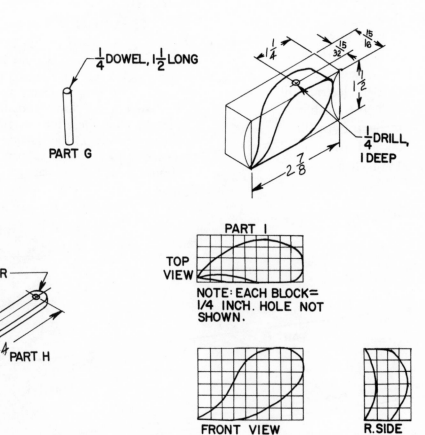

NOTE: EACH BLOCK= 1/4 INCH. HOLE NOT SHOWN.

Dump Truck

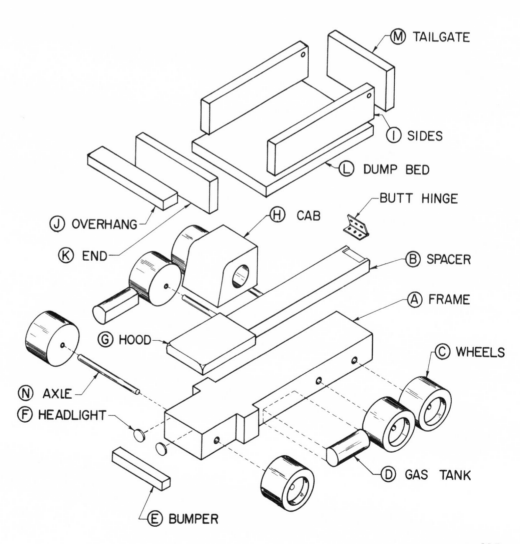

Ⓜ TAILGATE

Ⓘ SIDES

Ⓛ DUMP BED

BUTT HINGE

Ⓙ OVERHANG

Ⓚ END

Ⓗ CAB

Ⓑ SPACER

Ⓐ FRAME

Ⓖ HOOD

Ⓒ WHEELS

Ⓝ AXLE

Ⓕ HEADLIGHT

Ⓓ GAS TANK

Ⓔ BUMPER

MATERIALS

LETTER	NUMBER REQUIRED	NAME	SIZE
A	1	FRAME	11⅞ × 3¾ × 1⅛ inches
B	1	SPACER	8¼ × 1¹³⁄₁₆ × ½ inches
C	6	WHEEL	2½ × 2½ × 1½ inches
D	2	GAS TANK	1⅛-inch dowel, 2¼ inches long
E	1	BUMPER	3½ × ½ × ½ inches
F	2	HEADLIGHT	⅝ × ⅝ × ³⁄₁₆ inches
G	1	HOOD	2½ × 3⅝ × ½ inches
H	1	CAB	2½ × 2¾ × 2¼ inches
I	2	SIDE	7⅜ × 1⅞ × ½ inches
J	1	OVERHANG	5¼ × 1 × ½ inches
K	1	END	5¼ × 2¾ × ½ inches
L	1	BED	5¼ × 7⅞ × ½ inches
M	1	TAILGATE	4³⁄₁₆ × 2⅛ × ½ inches
N	3	AXLE	¼-inch dowel, 4¼ inches long

One 1 × 2 butt hinge
Two No. 6 finishing nails
Two No. 4 finishing nails
Three 1-inch wire brads
Twelve 1¼ × 10 flat head
  screws
Two 1 × 8 round head wood
  screws

TOOLS

C-clamps
Hammer
Nail set
Try square
1-inch wood chisel
Standard screwdriver
Wood file
Ruler
Coping saw
Jigsaw or band saw
Table saw

Electric drill
Disk or belt sander
No. 10 plug cutter
2½-inch hole saw
1½-inch spade bit
1½-inch Forstner bit
1¼ × 10 combination drill and
  countersink
³⁄₁₆-inch twist bit
⅜-inch twist bit

CONSTRUCTION NOTES

Frame, Spacer, Hood, and Cab Parts A, B, G, and H

Cut the frame, part A, using a jigsaw or a band saw. Drill the three holes required for the axles with a twist bit and an electric drill. Cut the spacer, part B, on the table saw. Glue and clamp part B to part A, so that part B is flush in the back and about ½ inch in from either side of part A.

Cut the hood, part G, with a table saw and round the corners with a wood file as shown. Cut the cab, part H, on a table saw and round its corners as shown with a wood file. Drill the hole in the cab, part H, using a spade bit. Glue part H, the cab, and part G, the hood, to the frame, part A. The front of the hood should be flush with the front of the frame; the back of the hood should touch the front of part B, the spacer. The back of the cab, part H, should be flush with the back of the hood, part G; parts H, G, and A should be flush on their sides.

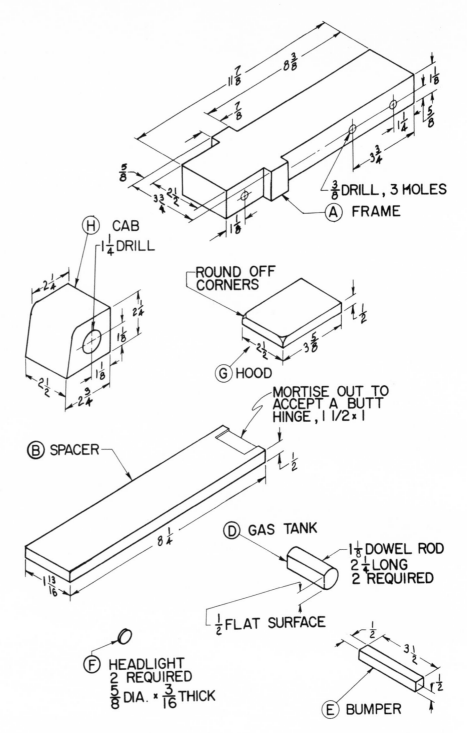

Gas Tank, Headlight, and Bumper Parts D, E, and F

Cut the gas tank, part D, from a piece of round molding, sand one side to a ½-inch flat surface on a disk or belt sander, and glue it to the frame, part A, so its back is 5¾ inches from the back of the frame. Also use a No. 6 finishing nail to attach it.

Cut the headlight, part F, from a dowel rod using a coping saw. Glue part F to the front of part A, the frame, and part G, the hood. With one wire brad attach each of them to the front of the truck. Part F, the headlight, should be ¼ inch from the sides and top of part A, the

frame, and part G, the hood. Cut the bumper, part E, on a table saw and nail it to the front of the frame, part A, with No. 4 finishing nails. Secure part E, the bumper, ⅛ inch above the bottom of part A. Part E, the bumper, should extend ½ inch on both sides of part A.

Wheel and Axle
Parts C and N

Cut the dowel rods for the axle, part N, using a coping saw. Use a hole saw and an electric drill to cut the wheels, part C. Use a Forstner bit to drill the centers. Slide the axle, part N, through the hole on part A, the frame. Glue the axle into the wheels. The axle should turn freely inside the hole in the frame, part A.

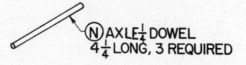

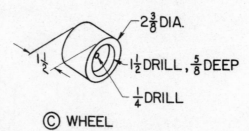

Bed
Parts I, J, K, L, and M

Resaw enough stock to make all the bed parts. Cut them to size on the table saw and drill the holes, with a twist bit and an electric drill, into the sides, part I. Attach part I, the sides, and part L, the bed, with glue and two screws from the bottom of part L, placing the screws approximately 2 inches from either end of part L. Part I, the sides, and part L, the bed, should be flush in back. Glue and screw on part K, the end, flush with the outsides of part I, the sides. Attach part K with three screws from the bottom of part L, the bed, one screw 1 inch in from either side and the third screw centered. Also place one screw on each side of the truck through part K, the end, into the side, part I. These screws should be 1½ inches up from the bottom of part L, the bed.

Glue the overhang, part J, to the end, part K, and use three screws equally spaced and driven through part K into part J. Part J, the overhang, and part K, the end, should be flush on top and sides. After attaching parts I, J, K, L, and M, cover the screws with a wooden plug made with a plug cutter in an electric drill.

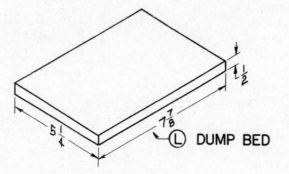

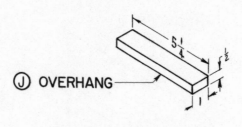

Place the tailgate, part M, in between the sides, part I, with top surfaces flush. Allow enough space (approximately 1/16 inch on the sides and bottom) for the tailgate to swing freely. Screw two round head screws into part M, the tailgate, leaving a loose fit between part M, the tailgate, and part I, the sides. Mortise out the space in the end of part L, the dump bed, and part B, the spacer, for a 1½-by-2 inch butt hinge, using a wood chisel. Attach the butt hinge so it is centered on the end of the spacer, part B, and also centered on the back portion of part L, the dump bed.

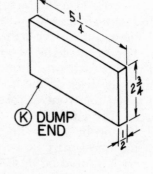

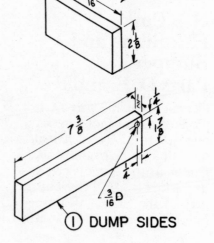

Earth Mover

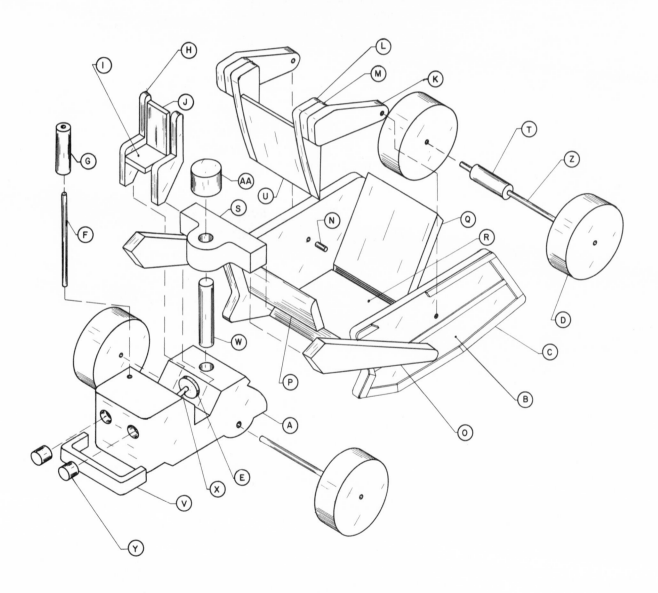

MATERIALS

LETTER	NUMBER REQUIRED	NAME	SIZE
A	1	FRONT END	9 × 3 × 4 inches
B	2	SIDE	13 × 5 × ½ inches
C	16	REINFORCEMENT BEAM	½ × ³⁄₁₆ × 50 inches
D	4	WHEEL	4⅜ × 4⅜ × 1½ inches
E	1	STEERING WHEEL	1⅜ round molding, ¼ inch long
F	1	EXHAUST PIPE	¼-inch dowel, 1½ inches long
G	1	MUFFLER	¾-inch dowel, 1½ inches long
H	2	SEAT SIDE	3 × 1½ × ¼ inches
I	1	SEAT BOTTOM	1 × 1 × ¼ inches
J	1	SEAT BACK	1¾ × 1 × ¼ inches
K	2	INFEED GATE ARM	6¾ × 1¾ × ½ inches
L	2	SCOOP SIDE	6¾ × 1½ × ½ inches
M	2	SPACER	1½ × 1¾ × ½ inches
N	2	INFEED GATE PIVOT	¼-inch dowel, 1 inch long
O	2	CONNECTER	9½ × 2 × ½ inches
P	1	SHORT ANGLED SIDE	5 × 1½ × ½ inches
Q	1	TALL ANGLED SIDE	4⅞ × 5 × ½ inches
R	1	BOTTOM	5 × 5 × ½ inches
S	1	PIVOT POST BRACKET	5 × 2½ × 1⅛ inches
T	1	SPACER	¾-inch dowel, 2⅛ inches long
U	1	SCOOP	5½ × 4⅛ × ⅝ inches
V	1	BUMPER	3½ × 1½ × ½ inches
W	1	PIVOT POST	¾-inch dowel, 3½ inches long
X	1	STEERING SHAFT	¼-inch dowel, 6 inches long
Y	2	HEADLIGHT	¾-inch dowel, ¾ inch long
Z	1	FRONT AXLE	¼-inch dowel, 6¼ inches long
—	1	REAR AXLE	¼-inch dowel, 6 inches long
AA	1	PIVOT CAP	1½ × 1½ × 1⅛ inches

Forty 1-inch wire brads
Forty ½-inch wire brads
Six No. 4 finishing nails

TOOLS

Hammer
Coping saw
Nail set
Wood file: smooth
Try square
Block plane
Ruler
Lathe
Lathe tools
Band saw
Table saw or radial arm saw
Electric drill
¼-inch twist bit
⅜-inch twist bit
¾-inch spade bit
1¾-inch hole saw

CONSTRUCTION NOTES

Front End
Parts A, E, V, X, and Y

Part A, the front end, should be glued from two 10-inch long pieces of 2-by-6 wood. Drill the 1-inch deep hole for the exhaust pipe, part F, using an electric drill and a twist bit. Drill the two ¾-inch holes for the headlights, part Y, using an electric drill and a spade bit; these should be ½ inch deep. Next, drill the ⅜-inch hole for the axle, part Z. Lay out and cut the contour shown in the top view, then lay out and cut the contour shown in the front view. Drill the ¼-inch diameter hole, ¾ inch deep, for the steering shaft, part X. Drill the ¾-inch diameter hole, 1½ inches deep, for the pivot post, part W.

Cut part Y, the headlights, and glue them into part A, the front end. They should protrude about ¼ inch. Part V, the bumper, must be cut to match the contour of the front of part A. If part A, the front end, varies slightly from specifications, the best method to match parts V and A is to trace the contour of part A. Then lay out the rest of part V and cut it, using the coping saw. Glue part V, the bumper, to part A, the front end, and nail ½-inch wire brads ¼ inch from the bottom of part A.

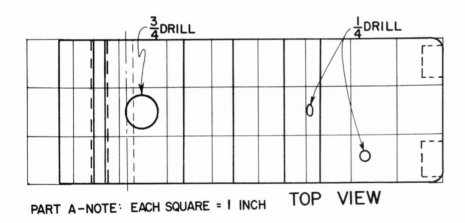

PART A-NOTE: EACH SQUARE = 1 INCH   TOP VIEW

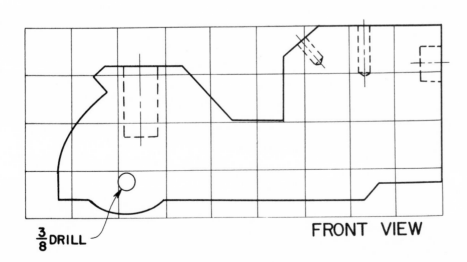

FRONT VIEW

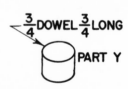

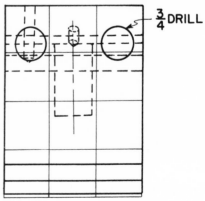

RIGHT SIDE VIEW

Cut part E, the steering wheel, and part X, the steering shaft, to their correct lengths using a coping saw. Drill the hole in part E with a twist bit and an electric drill. Glue part X, the steering shaft, into part A with ¾ inch protruding. Glue the steering wheel, part E, so part E and part X are flush on top.

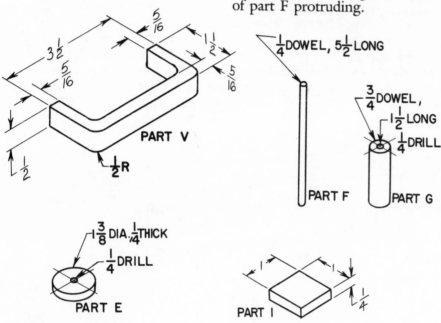

PART V

PART E

Seat
Parts H, I, and J

Cut part I, the seat bottom, part H, the seat sides, and part J, the seat back, with a coping saw. Glue part J to part H so they are flush in the back and part J is ¼ inch below the top of part H, and nail with 1-inch wire brads. Glue and nail part I, the seat bottom, to the sides, part H, so parts J and I touch and are square with each other. Once parts H, I, and J are assembled as one unit attach them to part A with glue and two 1-inch wire brads through the back portion of the seat bottom, part I.

Exhaust Pipe and Muffler
Parts F and G

Cut parts F and G, the exhaust pipe and muffler, to their correct lengths using a coping saw. Drill the hole through part G, the muffler, with a twist bit and an electric drill. Glue part G to part F, letting ½ inch of part F protrude. Glue part F into part A, the front end, leaving 4¾ inches of part F protruding.

¼ DOWEL, 5½ LONG

PART F

¾ DOWEL, 1½ LONG
¼ DRILL

PART G

PART I

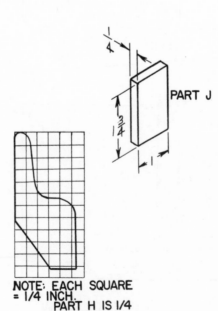

PART J

NOTE: EACH SQUARE = 1/4 INCH.
PART H IS 1/4 THICK.

Back Section
Parts B, C, O, P, Q, R, and S

Cut parts B, Q, R, P, and O on a table saw, radial arm saw, or coping saw. Drill the ¼-inch diameter holes in part B for the axle, part Z, and the ¼-inch hole for part K. Cut the angles on part Q with a table saw or radial arm saw. Glue and nail with 1-inch wire brads part R, the bottom, to part B, the side, so the end of part R touches part Q and the bottom of part R is flush with the bottom of part B. Glue and nail with 1-inch wire brads part Q to part B, the side. These should fit flush at the back and part Q should be at approximately a 45-degree angle to part R, as shown in the drawing. Glue and nail part P to part B. Round the corners of part P to match the contour of part B with a file. With the back section assembled into its frame attach part O by gluing and nailing with 1-inch wire brads at an angle of about 30 degrees, leaving 4 inches of part O extending past part B.

Cut approximately 50 inches of stock for the reinforcement beams, part C. These should be glued to the sides of part B as shown and nailed with ½-inch wire brads. Do not glue the strip covering the axle so that if the axle breaks while being played with the strip can easily be removed to replace the broken axle. The angles can easily be sanded to an exact fit with a small disk sander, or cut with a radial arm saw, table saw, or miter box saw. Cut out part S and drill a hole through it. Then glue part S to part O so part S is parallel with the ground and nail with 4 finishing nails.

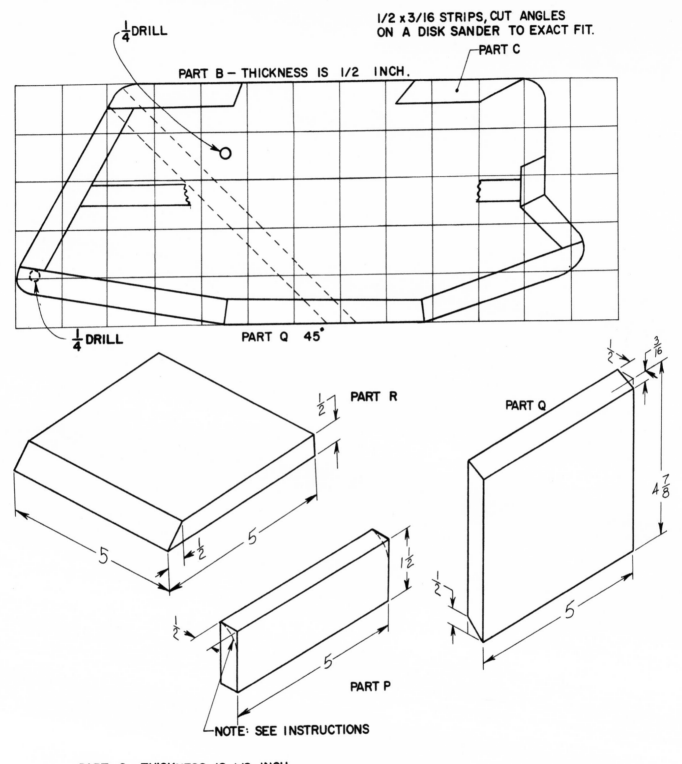

1/2 x 3/16 STRIPS, CUT ANGLES
ON A DISK SANDER TO EXACT FIT.

PART C

1/4 DRILL

PART B — THICKNESS IS 1/2 INCH.

1/4 DRILL

PART Q   45°

PART R

PART Q

PART P

NOTE: SEE INSTRUCTIONS

PART O , THICKNESS IS 1/2 INCH

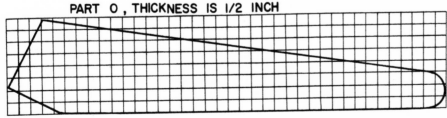

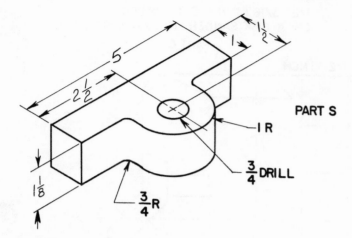

PART S

1 R

¾ DRILL

¾ R

Pivot Post and Cap
Parts W and AA

Cut the pivot post, part W, to length. Cut the pivot cap, part AA, using a 1¾-inch hole saw and an electric drill. Drill the hole in the bottom of part AA. Glue part W into part A, the front end. Slide part S over part W, but be sure not to let any glue get on parts S and W where they need to pivot. Glue the pivot cap, part AA, onto part W; part AA should fit firmly on part S so part S will rotate smoothly.

Infeed Gate
Parts K, L, M, N, and U

Cut parts K, M, and L using a coping saw. Drill a ¼-inch hole in part K. Attach parts K, L, and M, using glue and 1-inch wire brads, with tops flush, as shown in the exploded drawing. Cut the contour of part U, the scoop, with a block plane or a file; it should match the contour of part L. Glue and nail, using 1-inch wire brads, part U to part L. Once the infeed gate is completed it should fit down into the back section and pivot on the dowel, part N. Glue part N into part K but allow it to pivot in part B. Be sure no glue gets in the pivot hole in part B.

NOTE: EACH SQUARE = ¼ INCH

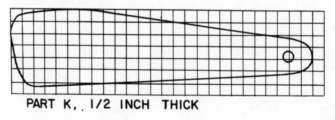

PART K, 1/2 INCH THICK

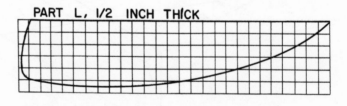

PART L, 1/2 INCH THICK

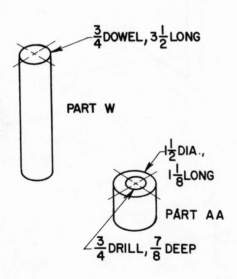

¾ DOWEL, 3½ LONG

PART W

1½ DIA., 1⅛ LONG

PART AA

¾ DRILL, ⅞ DEEP

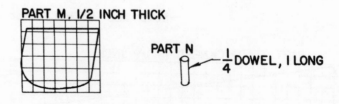

PART M, 1/2 INCH THICK

PART N — ¼ DOWEL, 1 LONG

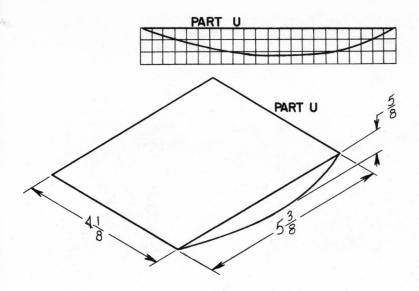

PART U

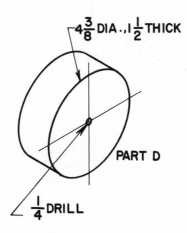

Wheel
Parts D, T, and Z

The four wheels, part D, should be turned on a wood lathe. Drill the holes for the axle, part Z. Cut the axles, part Z, to the proper lengths: note that the rear and front axles are different lengths. Cut part T, the spacer, and drill the center hole with a twist bit and an electric drill.

To assemble the front wheels slide the front axle through the hole on part A, then glue the axle to the wheels. The axle should rotate inside the hole on part A. To assemble the rear wheels slide the axle, part Z, through the hole on part B, glue on the two wheels, with the spacer, part T, in between. Allow the axle to turn inside the hole in part B.

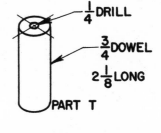

NOTE:
PART Z NOT SHOWN,
1/4 DOWEL FOR AXLE,
REAR AXLE 6 INCHES LONG,
FRONT AXLE 6 1/4.

Road Roller

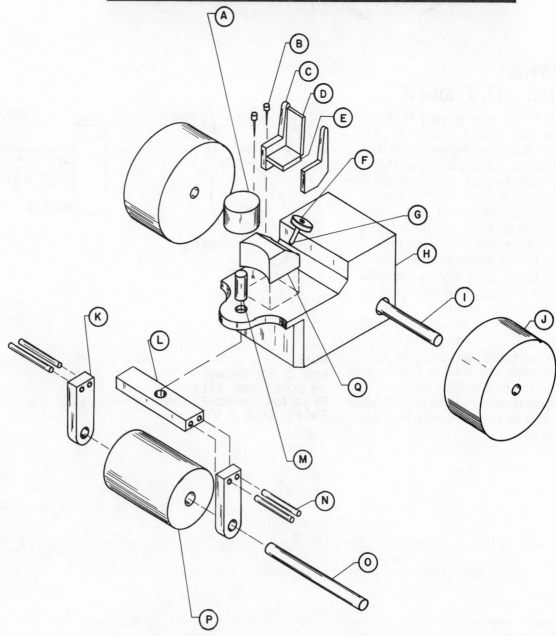

MATERIALS

LETTER	NUMBER REQUIRED	NAME	SIZE
A	1	FRONT CYLINDER	1½ × 1½ × 1⅛ inches
B	2	CONTROL KNOB	¼-inch dowel, ¼ inch long
C	2	SEAT SIDE	2 × 1¼ × 1¼ inches
D	1	SEAT BACK	1 × ⅞ × ¼ inches
E	1	SEAT BOTTOM	⅞ × ¾ × 3/16 inches
F	1	STEERING WHEEL	1⅜-inch round molding, ¼ inch long
G	1	STEERING COLUMN	¼-inch dowel, 1¼ inches long
H	1	BODY	8 × 4 × 4 inches
I	1	REAR AXLE	½-inch dowel, 8½ inches long
J	2	REAR WHEEL	4½ × 4½ × 2 inches
K	2	ROLLER WHEEL BRACKET	3 1/16 × 1⅛ × ½ inches
L	1	ROLLER WHEEL FRAME	4¼ × 1⅛ × ½ inches
M	1	SHORT CONNECTING POST	½-inch dowel, 1⅞ inches long
N	4	LONG CONNECTING POST	¼-inch dowel, 1½ inches long
O	1	FRONT AXLE	½-inch dowel, 5¼ inches long
P	1	ROLLER WHEEL	2¾ × 2¾ × 4 inches long
Q	1	DASHBOARD	2 × 2 × 1⅛ inches

Four No. 4 finishing nails
Eight 1-inch wire brads

TOOLS

Pliers
Clamps
Hammer
Try square
Compass
Ruler
Coping saw
Table saw
Band saw
Electric drill
¾-inch spade bit
½-inch spade bit
¼-inch twist bit
1/16-inch twist bit
5/8-inch spade bit
1¾-inch hole saw

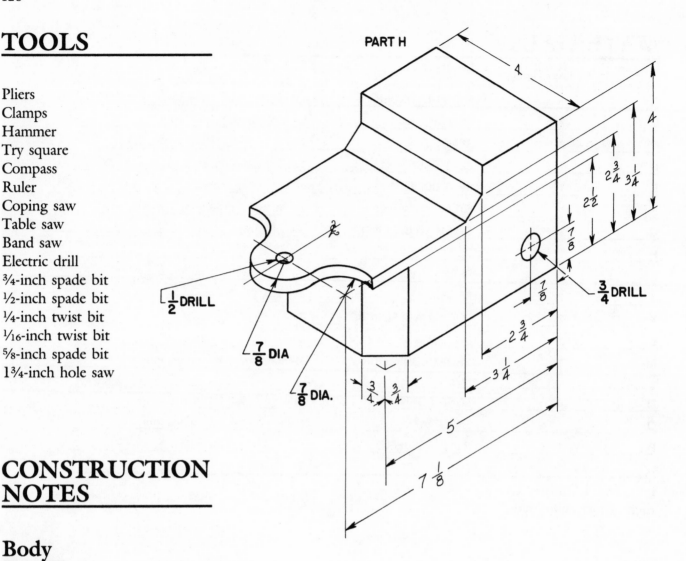

CONSTRUCTION NOTES

Body
Part H

The body, part H, should be glued from 2-by-6 stock. Use a band saw to cut the shape of part H. Drill the hole through the stock for the axles, parts I and O, and for part M, using a spade bit and an electric drill.

Dashboard, Steering Wheel, and Control Knob
Parts B, F, G, and Q

Cut part Q, the dashboard, with a band saw. Drill the hole for the steering column, part G, with an electric drill and a twist bit. Glue and nail with finishing nails the dashboard, part Q, to the body, part H, leaving 1 inch on both sides; the inside of the curved section should be 1⅝ inches from the front of the body, part H.

Cut part G, the steering column, and part F, the steering wheel, using a band saw. Glue part G, the steering column, into the hole in part Q, the dashboard, so part G protrudes from part Q ¾ inch. Glue part F, the steering wheel, onto part G, the steering column, so they are flush on top.

Cut part B, the control knobs, using a band saw. Drill a 1/16-inch hole halfway through one end of the control knob, using an electric drill and a 1/16-inch twist bit. Using a hammer, drive two finishing nails ½ inch apart, ⅜ inch in from one side, and ¼ inch back from the dashboard, part Q. Cut the nail's head off with pliers. Glue the control knobs, part B, onto the nails.

PART B – $\frac{1}{4}$ DOWEL, $\frac{1}{4}$ LONG

PART F – $1\frac{3}{8}$ ROUND MOLDING,

$\frac{1}{4}$ LONG, $\frac{1}{4}$ DRILL IN CENTER

PART G – $\frac{1}{4}$ DOWEL, $1\frac{1}{4}$ LONG

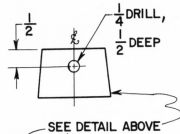

$\frac{1}{2}$

$\frac{1}{4}$ DRILL, $\frac{1}{2}$ DEEP

SEE DETAIL ABOVE

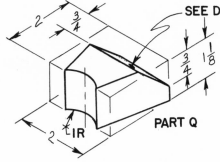

2

$\frac{3}{4}$

$\frac{3}{4}$ $1\frac{1}{8}$

2

1R

PART Q

Rear Wheel Parts I and J

Turn part J, the rear wheels, on a wood lathe, and drill the ½-inch hole with a twist bit and an electric drill. Cut part I, the rear axle, using a coping saw. Slide the rear axle, part I, through the hole in part H, the body, and glue the wheels, part J, onto the rear axle, part I, keeping the ends of part I flush with the outside of part J.

PART I – $\frac{1}{2}$ DOWEL, $8\frac{1}{2}$ LONG

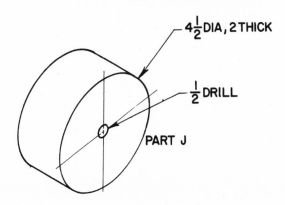

$4\frac{1}{2}$ DIA, 2 THICK

$\frac{1}{2}$ DRILL

PART J

Seat Parts C, D, and E

Cut part D, the seat back, and part E, the seat bottom, using a table saw. Part C, the seat side, is ¼ inch thick and should be cut with the table saw and coping saw. Glue and nail the seat back, part D, to the seat sides, part C, with their backs flush. The top of the seat back, part D, should be ⅛ inch below the top of the seat sides, part C. Glue and nail the seat bottom, part E, to the seat sides, part C. The bottom of the seat bottom, part E, should be ½ inch up from the bottom of the sides, part C; the fronts of parts E and C should be flush.

Once the seat is assembled, nail it to the body, part H, through the seat sides, part C, using two finishing nails. The back of the seat should touch the body, part H, and be 1⅛ inches from both sides of the body.

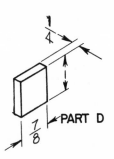

PART C

NOTE: EACH SQUARE = $\frac{1}{4}$ INCH

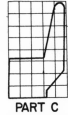

$\frac{1}{4}$

$\frac{7}{8}$ ← PART D

PART E

$\frac{3}{16}$ $\frac{7}{8}$

$\frac{3}{4}$

Wheel Support Mechanism Parts A, K, L, M, and N

Choose a piece of stock large enough to make part A and cut it to a thickness of 1⅛ inches. Cut part A with a 1¾-inch hole saw and an electric drill. Drill the required hole with a twist bit and an electric drill.

$1\frac{1}{2}$ DIA., $1\frac{1}{8}$ LONG

PART A

$\frac{1}{2}$ DRILL, $1\frac{1}{4}$ DEEP

Cut part L, using a table saw. Drill the large hole and the four small holes in part L with an electric drill and appropriate twist bits. Cut part K, using the table saw and a coping saw. Drill the hole for the front axle, part O, and the two holes for part N, using the electric drill and proper sizes of twist bits. Cut part M using a coping saw. Glue and clamp part N into the holes in part K and part L. Part K and part L should be flush on top and sides. The ends of the dowels, part N, should be flush with the outside of part K. Place part M through the hole in part H. Do not glue. Part M should be glued into part L, with bottoms flush, and should turn smoothly in part H.

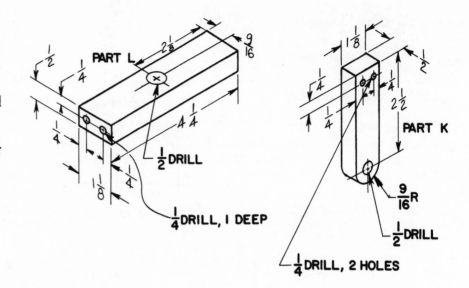

PART M – $\frac{1}{2}$ DOWEL, $1\frac{7}{8}$ LONG

PART N – $\frac{1}{4}$ DOWEL, $1\frac{1}{2}$ LONG

Roller Wheel
Parts O and P

Part P, the roller wheel, must be turned on a wood lathe. Drill the hole with a spade bit and an electric drill. Cut part O, the front axle, using a coping saw. Glue part O, the front axle, in the hole in part K, letting part P, the roller wheel, rotate freely on part O, the front axle.

PART O – $\frac{1}{2}$ DOWEL, $5\frac{1}{4}$ LONG

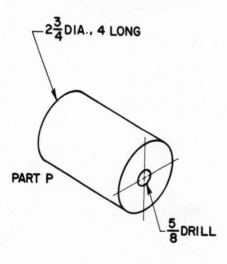

PART P

Dozer

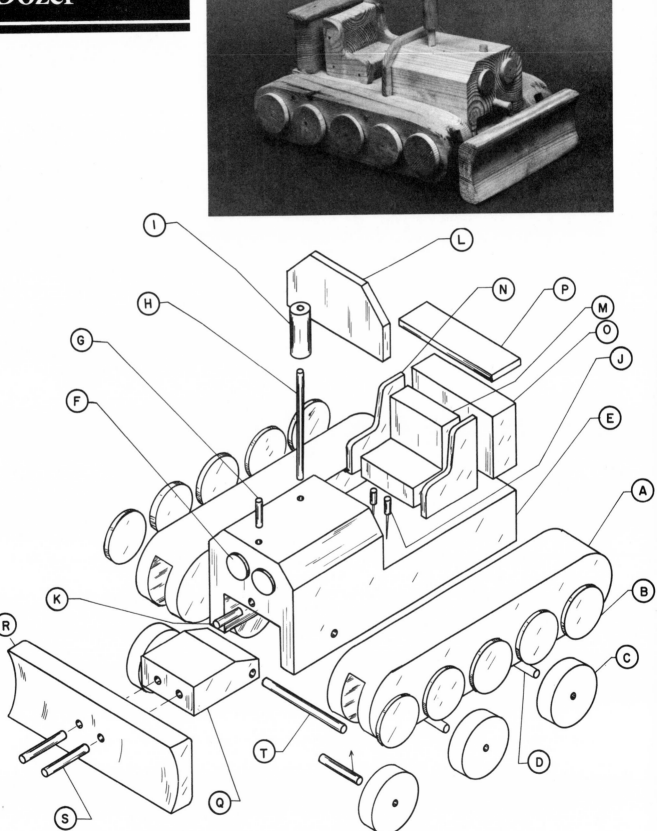

MATERIALS

LETTER	NUMBER REQUIRED	NAME	SIZE
A	2	TRACK	7⁵⁄₁₆ × 1⅞ × 1⅜ inches
B	5	TRACK ROLLER	1⅜-inch round molding, ³⁄₁₆ inch thick
C	6	WHEEL	1⅝ × 1⅝ × ⁹⁄₁₆ inches
D	6	AXLE	¼-inch dowel, 1¼ inches long
E	1	FRAME	7½ × 2⅞ × 2¹³⁄₁₆ inches
F	2	HEADLIGHT	¾-inch dowel, ⅛ inch long
G	1	WATER CAP	¼-inch dowel, ¾ inch long
H	1	EXHAUST PIPE	¼-inch dowel, 3 inches long
I	1	MUFFLER	½-inch dowel, 1¼ inches long
J	2	CONTROL KNOB	¼-inch dowel, ⅜ inch long
K	1	BLADE LOCK	¼-inch dowel, 1⅝ inches long
L	1	DASHBOARD	3¼ × 1¾ × ¼ inches
M	1	SEAT	1¾ × 1⅝ × 1¾ inches
N	2	SEAT SIDE	2 × 2 × ⅛ inches
O	1	GAS TANK	2¾ × ⅝ × 1¾ inches
P	1	GAS TANK LID	3⅛ × ¹⁵⁄₁₆ × ³⁄₁₆ inches
Q	1	BLADE SUPPORT	2¼ × 1¾ × ¾ inches
R	1	BLADE	5½ × 1⅞ × ¾ inches
S	2	BLADE ROD	¼-inch dowel, 1⅜ inches long
T	1	BLADE SUPPORT ROD	¼-inch dowel, 2¾ inches long

Four 10 *d* finishing nails
Thirty-one wire brads
Two No. 4 finishing nails
Ten ½-inch wire brads

TOOLS

C-clamp   Table saw
Hammer   Drum sander
Ruler   Band saw
Nail set   Electric drill
Wood file   ¼-inch twist bit
Coping saw   1¾-inch hole saw

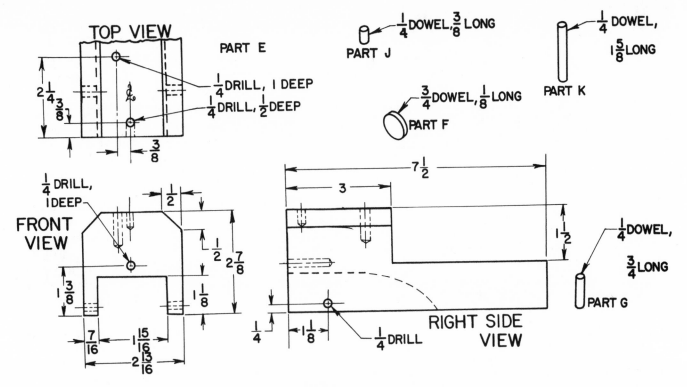

CONSTRUCTION NOTES

Frame Parts E, F, G, J, K, and L

Glue two pieces of 2-by-4 board, 8 inches long. Cut this laminated piece to the finished length for part E, the frame, on a table saw. On the table saw cut the angles shown on the front view, the full length of the dozer. Turn the frame over and cut a groove on the bottom by cutting a series of saw kerfs on the table saw. Next cut the shape shown on the right side view, also with the table saw.

Drill the holes for the water cap, part G, the exhaust pipe, part H, the blade lock, part K, and the blade support rod, part T. Cut parts G, K, and J with a coping saw. Glue part G, the water cap, into the frame, part E, leaving ⅛ inch protruding.

Fit part K, the blade lock, into the hole on the front of part E, but do not glue: this will allow part K to slide in and out and to hold the blade or drop it.

Drill a 1/16-inch hole halfway into the control knobs, part J, from the bottom so a wire brad can be fitted. Drive the wire brads into the dozer frame 3⅝ inches from the back and 1 inch from each side. Cut off the heads of the wire brads and glue the control knobs, part J, onto them.

Cut part L with a coping saw and attach part L to the frame, part E, with glue and two wire brads from the back. The dash, part L, should overhang the dozer frame, part E, by ¼ inch on all sides but the bottom.

Cut two thin disks, using a coping saw, from a dowel rod for part F, the headlights. Glue and nail part F onto the front of part E, the frame, with one wire brad in the center. The edge of part F should be ½ inch from the side and about ⅜ inch from the top.

Seat
Parts M and N

Cut two pieces for part N, the seat sides, with a coping saw. Cut the seat, part M, on a table saw by holding a board at least 1 foot long and cutting a notch for the seat. Several cuts may be required. The reason for a foot-long board is to keep fingers a safe distance away from the blade. After the notch is cut in part M, cut the seat to the correct size on the table saw. Glue part N, the seat sides, to part M, the seat, and nail with wire brads. They should be flush on the back and bottom. Nail, with two No. 4 finishing nails, the seat to the dozer frame, part E, so the back is 1¼ inches from the back of the frame, centered from side to side.

Gas Tank
Parts P and O

The gas tank, part O, and the gas tank lid, part P, can be cut easily on a table saw. With wire brads, glue and nail the gas tank lid, part P, to the gas tank, part O. The gas tank lid should overlap the tank all the way around by about ⅛ inch. Glue and clamp the gas tank and the gas tank lid to the frame, part E, with the gas tank, part O, ⅛ inch from the back of the frame, part E, and centered from side to side.

Blade
Parts Q, R, S, and T

The cove or curved part of the blade, part R, can be made on a table saw (see Cutting a Cove in the chapter titled Helpful Hints), filed with a wood file, or sanded with a drum sander. After the cove is done, drill the two holes for part S and the hole in the back of the blade with a twist bit and an electric drill. Cut part Q, the blade support, on the table saw, drilling the holes with a twist bit and an electric drill. Cut part T and part S with a coping saw. Assemble by gluing part S into part R, the blade, and part Q, the blade support. Clamp these together to hold the parts together tightly until the glue dries. Once parts S, R, and Q are assembled, slide part T through the frame, part E, and into the blade support, part Q. Glue is not required since part T is covered by the track, part A.

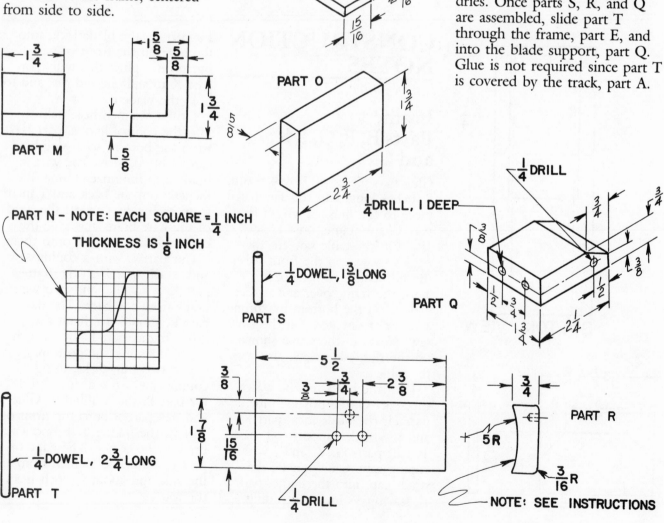

Track and Wheel Parts A, B, C, and D

Make part A, the track, by cutting a piece of stock 16 by 1⅞ by 1⅜ inches, using a table saw. Cut several dado cuts, each one about ¼ inch deeper, until the required depth is reached. The 16-inch long piece is safer than two 8-inch pieces. Lay out the shape of the track and cut it with a band saw. Drill the three holes on the track, part A, for the axle, part D, using an electric drill and a twist bit.

Slice a piece of round molding for the track rollers, part B; use a table saw. Cut part C, the wheels, using a 1¾-inch diameter hole saw and an electric drill. Cut part D, the axles, with a coping saw.

To assemble parts A, B, C, and D, slide part D into the holes on the track, part A, and through the wheels, part C, which are inside the dado cuts in the track, part A. Once parts A, C, and D are assembled, glue and nail the track rollers, part B, to the track. These should be spaced equally along the center of the track, with about ¼ inch of space between them. Once parts A, B, C, and D are assembled into one unit attach them to the frame, part E, with two No. 10 finishing nails. Drill small holes for these nails to prevent them from breaking the tracks when they are attached. The top of the track, part A, should be flush with the center surface of part E, the frame (the surface the seat, part M, is attached to). The track, part A, should hang over part E on each end by approximately ⅜ inch.

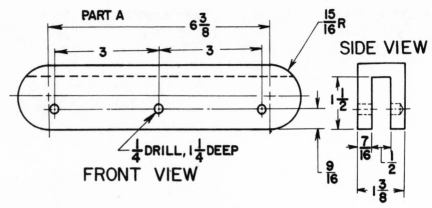

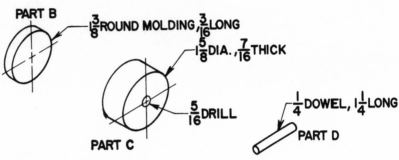

Exhaust Pipe and Muffler Parts H and I

Using a coping saw cut parts H and I to the correct lengths. Drill all the way through part I, the muffler, with a twist bit and an electric drill. Glue the muffler, part I, onto the exhaust pipe, part H, leaving ¼ inch of the exhaust pipe protruding from the muffler. The exhaust pipe should extend from the dozer about 2 inches.

½ DOWEL, 1¼ LONG — PART I, ¼ DRILL

¼ DOWEL, 3 LONG — PART H

Grader

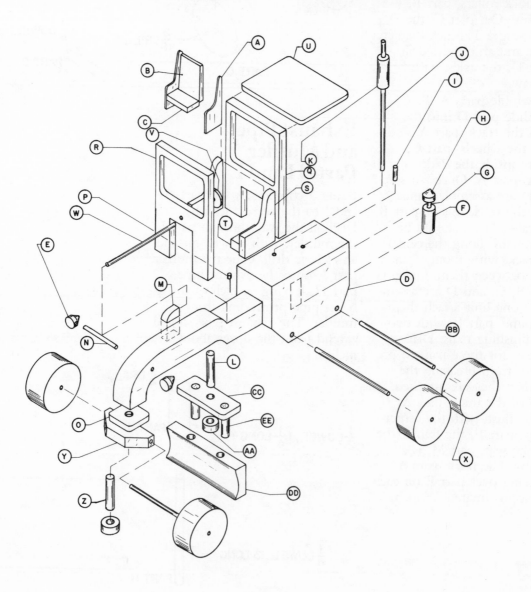

MATERIALS

LETTER	NUMBER REQUIRED	NAME	SIZE
A	2	SEAT SIDE	3¼ × 1½ × ¼ inches
B	1	SEAT BACK	1¾ × 2⅜ × ¼ inches
C	1	SEAT BOTTOM	1¾ × ⅞ × ½ inches
D	1	FRAME	18 × 4¾ × 2⅞ inches
E	2	HEADLIGHT	¾-inch dowel, ¾ inch long
F	1	AIR FILTER	¾-inch dowel, 1¼ inches long
G	1	AIR FILTER PIPE	¼-inch dowel, 1½ inches long
H	1	AIR FILTER CAP	¾-inch dowel, ⅝ inch long
I	1	GAS CAP	¼-inch dowel, ¾ inch long
J	1	EXHAUST PIPE	¼-inch dowel, 6½ inches long
K	1	MUFFLER	¾-inch dowel, 2¼ inches long
L	1	BLADE PIVOT POST	½-inch dowel, 2 inches long
M	1	STEERING BOX	1⅛ × ½ × ⅝ inches
N	1	HEADLIGHT SUPPORT	¼-inch dowel, 3⅛ inches long
O	1	SPACER	1¾ × 2 × ¼ inches
P	1	GEAR KNOB	¼-inch dowel, ¼ inch long
Q	1	CAB BACK	7½ × 4½ × ½ inches
R	1	CAB FRONT	7½ × 4½ × ½ inches
S	2	CAB SIDE	2½ × 3½ × ½ inches
T	2	CAB BOTTOM	3½ × 15⁄16 × ½ inches
U	1	CAB TOP	4 × 5 × ¼ inches
V	1	STEERING WHEEL	1⅜-inch round molding, ¼ inch long
W	1	STEERING SHAFT	¼-inch dowel, 5 inches long
X	6	WHEEL	3½ × 3½ × 1½ inches
Y	1	AXLE HOUSING	3 × 1½ × ¾ inches
Z	1	FRONT PIVOT POST	½-inch dowel, 2½ inches long
AA	2	LOCKING DEVICE	1½ × 1½ × ⅝ inches
BB	3	AXLE	¼-inch dowel, 6¼ inches long
CC	1	BRACKET	3⅞ × 1½ × ½ inches
DD	1	BLADE	6 × 1½ × ¾ inches
EE	2	BLADE SUPPORT	½-inch dowel, 3⅝ inches long

Thirty 1-inch wire brads

TOOLS

Ruler
Pencil
Hammer
Coping saw
Clamps
Try square
Nail set
Wood file or wood rasp
Lathe
Lathe tools
Band saw
Electric hand drill
Table saw
Belt sander or drum sander
1¾-inch hole saw
1/16-inch twist bit
3/8-inch twist bit
¼-inch twist bit
½-inch twist bit

CONSTRUCTION NOTES

Frame
Part D

The frame is made from two 2-by-6 inch pieces of stock, 18 inches long. They are glued together (laminated), using C-clamps, to make one piece of wood. Avoid using pieces with large defects.

After laminating the stock, cut the contour shown on the front view using a band saw. Drill the two holes for the axle with a 3/8-inch twist bit and an electric drill. Then drill the holes for the exhaust pipe and muffler, gas cap, and headlights. Once the holes have been drilled, lay out and cut the contour on the top view. Then drill with a twist bit the hole for part Z, the front pivot post, and part L, the blade pivot post. Sand the frame smooth before attaching any other parts.

Muffler and Exhaust Pipe Parts J and K

Carefully drill the hole into the center of part K, using a twist bit and an electric drill. Part K may break easily during this operation, so repeated attempts may be necessary. Glue part J into part K—no clamps are required. Leave about 1 inch of part J protruding from the top of part K, and glue part J into the frame, part D.

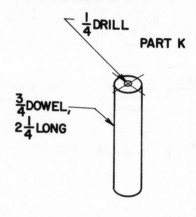

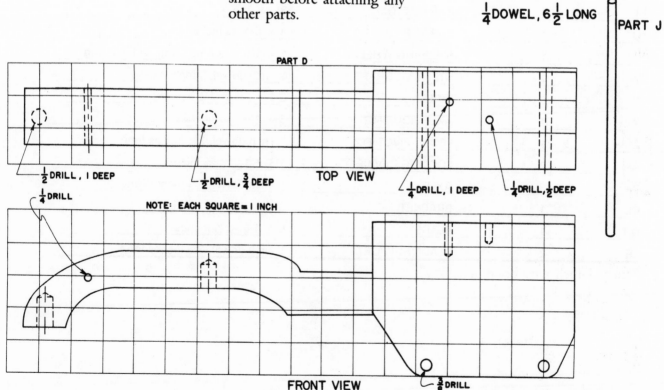

Air Filter
Parts F, G, and H

Part H should initially be 6 to 8 inches long to make it easier and safer to hold. Sand the cone-shaped top of part H before cutting it to its final length. Cut parts F and H to the proper lengths, using a coping saw. Sand or file a flat spot on one side of part F, from top to bottom, with a wood file or belt sander. Drill the holes in parts H and F for part G. Assemble and glue parts H, G, and F, leaving about ¾ inch between parts H and F. Glue the flat part of part F onto the frame. Secure the air filter with two wire brads; predrill holes through the hardwood dowels so the wire brads will not bend.

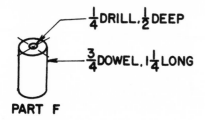

¼ DOWEL, 1½ LONG

PART G

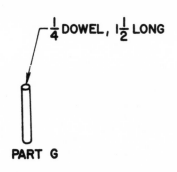

¼ DRILL, ½ DEEP

¾ DOWEL, 1¼ LONG

PART F

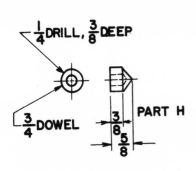

¼ DRILL, ⅜ DEEP

¾ DOWEL

⅜ ⅝

PART H

Gas Cap
Part I

The gas cap should protrude from the frame about ¼ inch. Sand one end to a dome shape. Glue the cap into the frame.

¼ DOWEL,
¾ LONG

PART I

Headlight
Parts E and N

Sand the cone-shaped ends on both ends of part E, a dowel rod that is initially 6 to 8 inches long, with a belt sander or by hand. Drill the holes with a twist bit into part E to accept part N. Cut part E into 2 pieces of the proper length. Glue part N into the frame and then glue the headlights, part E, onto each end of part N.

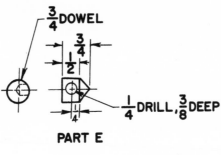

¾ DOWEL

¾

½

¼

¼ DRILL, ⅜ DEEP

PART E

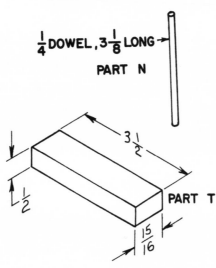

¼ DOWEL, 3⅛ LONG

PART N

3½

½

15/16

PART T

Cab
Parts P, Q, R, S, T, and U

Plane or resaw with a band saw or jointer enough stock to make parts Q, R, S, and T to the dimensions shown. Cut parts Q, R, S, and T with a coping saw or jigsaw. Drill the hole in part R with a twist bit. Glue and nail the parts together, using wire brads. The bottoms and sides of parts Q, R, and S should fit flush. Part T is fitted onto Q, R, and S about 1 inch from their bottoms.

Next cut part U and attach it to parts Q and R with glue and wire brads, allowing part U to hang over about ¼ inch on all sides.

Cut part P, the gear knob, to length with a coping saw and round by sanding all over. Drill halfway into it with a bit the same diameter as a wire brad. Next, drive a wire brad into the frame ½ inch in front of where the seat, parts A, B, and C, will be located. Cut the head off the nail, using needle nose pliers, and glue part P onto it.

The cab, parts Q, R, S, T, and U, already assembled, can now be attached to the frame. Glue part T to the frame. Nail part Q to the frame with wire brads.

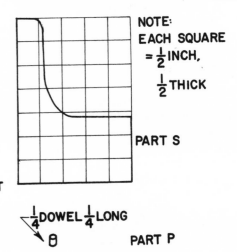

NOTE:
EACH SQUARE
= ½ INCH.

½ THICK

PART S

¼ DOWEL ¼ LONG

PART P

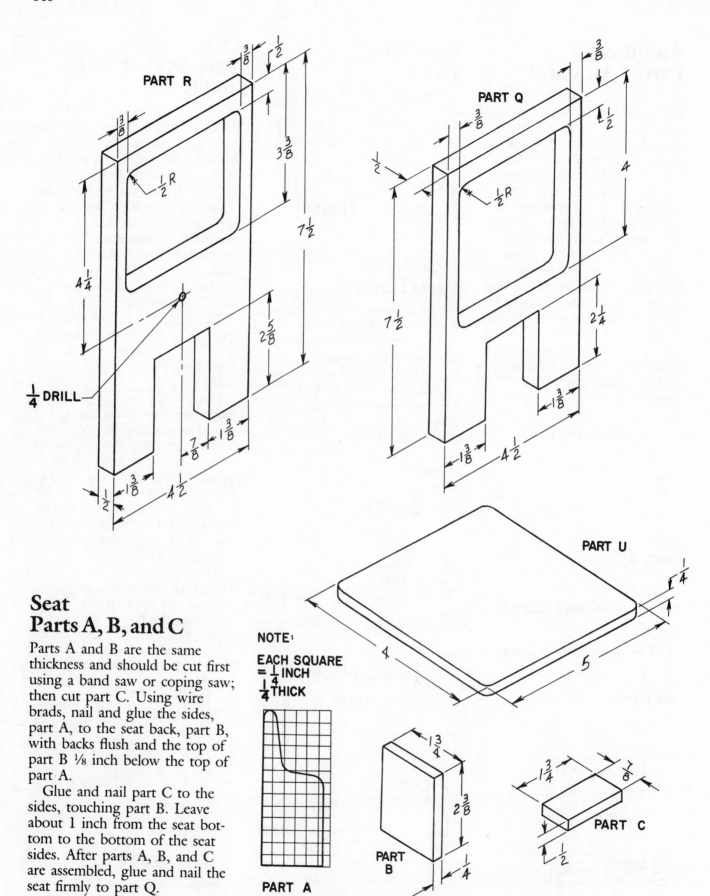

PART R

PART Q

PART U

½ R

¼ DRILL

Seat
Parts A, B, and C

Parts A and B are the same thickness and should be cut first using a band saw or coping saw; then cut part C. Using wire brads, nail and glue the sides, part A, to the seat back, part B, with backs flush and the top of part B ⅛ inch below the top of part A.

Glue and nail part C to the sides, touching part B. Leave about 1 inch from the seat bottom to the bottom of the seat sides. After parts A, B, and C are assembled, glue and nail the seat firmly to part Q.

NOTE:
EACH SQUARE
= ¼ INCH
¼ THICK

PART A

PART B

PART C

Steering
Parts M, V, and W

Cut the dowel, part W, to length. Then cut and sand the steering wheel, part V, on the band saw. Cut part M, the steering box. Drill the hole in part M with a twist bit, then sand. Insert part W into the hole in the steering box and glue it. Slide part W through the hole in part R, the cab front, so it protrudes 1 inch. Glue and nail part M, the steering box, to part D, the frame. Then glue part V, the steering wheel, onto part W, the steering shaft.

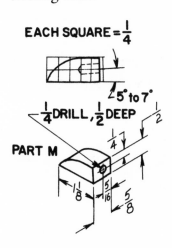

EACH SQUARE = $\frac{1}{4}$

5° to 7°

$\frac{1}{4}$ DRILL, $\frac{1}{2}$ DEEP

PART M

$\frac{1}{4}$

$\frac{1}{2}$

$\frac{1}{8}$ $\frac{5}{16}$ $\frac{5}{8}$

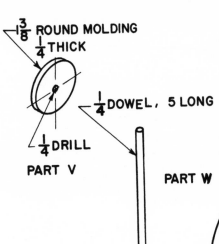

$\frac{3}{8}$ ROUND MOLDING

$\frac{1}{4}$ THICK

$\frac{1}{4}$ DOWEL, 5 LONG

$\frac{1}{4}$ DRILL

PART V

PART W

Wheel
Parts O, X, Y, Z, AA, and BB

Turn the six wheels, part X, required for both the front and back of the grader on the lathe to the appropriate dimensions. Cut the three axles, part BB, with a coping saw. Cut part O, the spacer, with a coping saw and drill the hole with a twist bit. Cut part Y, using a coping saw, and drill the holes for the front pivot post, part Z, and the axle, with a twist bit. Next cut part Z, the front pivot post, to length using a coping saw. Finally cut the two locking devices, part AA, using a 1¾-inch diameter hole saw; the second one is for the blade mechanism.

Glue and nail part O, the spacer, to the frame, part D. It should be ⅛ inch larger on all sides than the part of the frame onto which it fits. Next glue part Z, the front pivot post, into parts O and D, leaving 2 inches protruding from part O. Slide part Y onto part Z but *do not glue*. This will allow part Y to turn. Next glue the locking device, part AA, to part Z, to secure part Y. Then slide the axle, part BB, through the axle holes in parts Y and D. The axles should be free to rotate inside the holes, since the axles are smaller in diameter than the holes. Glue the wheels to the axles, flush outside.

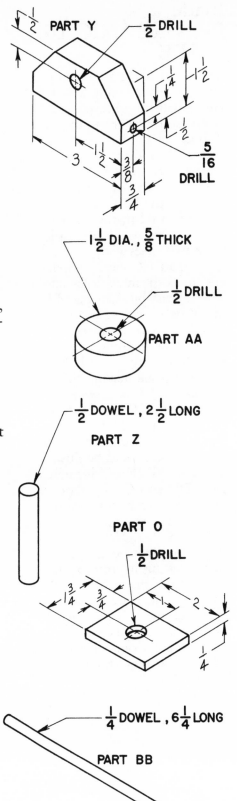

$\frac{1}{2}$ PART Y $\frac{1}{2}$ DRILL

$\frac{1}{4}$ $1\frac{1}{2}$

$\frac{1}{2}$

$\frac{5}{16}$ DRILL

$3\frac{1}{2}$ $\frac{3}{8}$ $\frac{3}{4}$

$1\frac{1}{2}$ DIA., $\frac{5}{8}$ THICK

$\frac{1}{2}$ DRILL

PART AA

$\frac{1}{2}$ DOWEL, $2\frac{1}{2}$ LONG

PART Z

PART O

$\frac{1}{2}$ DRILL

$\frac{3}{4}$ $\frac{3}{4}$ 1   2

$\frac{1}{4}$

$\frac{1}{4}$ DRILL

PART X

$3\frac{1}{2}$ DIA., $1\frac{1}{2}$ THICK

$\frac{1}{4}$ DOWEL, $6\frac{1}{4}$ LONG

PART BB

Blade
Parts L, AA, CC, DD, and EE

Begin by cutting a cove in part DD, the blade; using a table saw, a half round rasp, or a drum sander to create the cove. Round out the back contour with a block plane or rasp. Leave the top section of the blade its full ¾-inch thickness to allow room for the holes that accommodate part EE, the blade supports. Then lay out and drill these two holes with a twist bit.

Cut part CC with a coping saw and drill three holes into it with a twist bit. Cut part EE, the blade supports, and part L, the blade pivot post, to their correct length, using a coping saw. You should already have cut part AA while making the wheels.

Glue part EE, the blade supports, into part DD, the blade, and part CC, the bracket. Parts EE and CC should be flush on top. Part EE should separate parts DD and CC by about 2 inches, although this measurement may vary slightly from one toy to another. Next glue part L, the blade pivot post, into the frame, letting it protrude 1⅛ inches from the bottom. Slide part CC onto part L but *do not glue.* Leaving this piece free of glue allows the blade to turn. Glue part AA onto the bottom of part L to hold the blade in place.

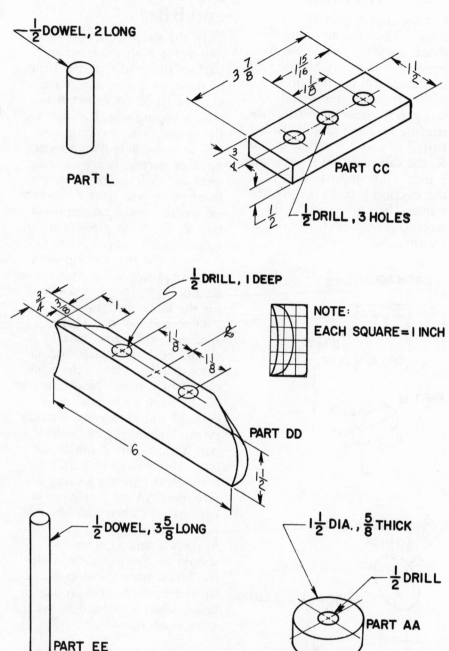

½ DOWEL, 2 LONG

PART L

3 7/8   1 15/16   1 1/8   1 ½

3/4

½

½ DRILL, 3 HOLES

PART CC

½ DRILL, I DEEP

NOTE:
EACH SQUARE = I INCH

3/4   3/8   1

1 1/8   1 1/8

6   1 ½

PART DD

½ DOWEL, 3 5/8 LONG

PART EE

1 ½ DIA., 5/8 THICK

½ DRILL

PART AA

Metric Conversion Table

INCHES	MILLIMETERS
1/32	.7938
1/16	1.5875
3/32	2.3813
1/8	3.175
5/32	3.9688
3/16	4.7625
7/32	5.5563
1/4	6.35
9/32	7.1438
5/16	7.9375
11/32	8.7313
3/8	9.525
13/32	10.3188
7/16	11.1125
15/32	11.9063
1/2	12.70
17/32	13.4938
9/16	14.2875
19/32	15.0813
5/8	15.875
21/32	16.6688
11/16	17.4625
23/32	18.2563
3/4	19.05
25/32	19.8438
13/16	20.6375
27/32	21.4313
7/8	22.225
29/32	23.0188
15/16	23.8125
31/32	24.6063
1	25.4001

METRIC SYSTEM

UNIT	ABBREVIATION		APPROXIMATE U.S. EQUIVALENT		
		Length			
		Number of Metres			
myriametre	mym	10,000	6.2 miles		
kilometre	km	1000	0.62 mile		
hectometre	hm	100	109.36 yards		
dekametre	dam	10	32.81 feet		
metre	m	1	39.37 inches		
decimetre	dm	0.1	3.94 inches		
centimetre	cm	0.01	0.39 inch		
millimetre	mm	0.001	0.04 inch		
		Area			
		Number of Square Metres			
square kilometre	sq km *or* km²	1,000,000	0.3861 square miles		
hectare	ha	10,000	2.47 acres		
are	a	100	119.60 square yards		
centare	ca	1	10.76 square feet		
square centimetre	sq cm *or* cm²	0.0001	0.155 square inch		
		Volume			
		Number of Cubic Metres			
dekastere	das	10	13.10 cubic yards		
stere	s	1	1.31 cubic yards		
decistere	ds	0.10	3.53 cubic feet		
cubic centimetre	cu cm *or* cm³ *also* cc	0.000001	0.061 cubic inch		

UNIT	ABBREVIATION	Number of Litres	Cubic	Dry	Liquid
		Capacity			
kilolitre	kl	1000	1.31 cubic yards		
hectolitre	hl	100	3.53 cubic feet	2.84 bushels	
dekalitre	dal	10	0.35 cubic foot	1.14 pecks	2.64 gallons
litre	l	1	61.02 cubic inches	0.908 quart	1.057 quarts
decilitre	dl	0.10	6.1 cubic inches	0.18 pint	0.21 pint
centilitre	cl	0.01	0.6 cubic inch		0.338 fluidounce
millilitre	ml	0.001	0.06 cubic inch		0.27 fluidram

UNIT	ABBREVIATION	Number of Grams	APPROXIMATE U.S. EQUIVALENT
		Mass and Weight	
metric ton	MT *or* t	1,000,000	1.1 tons
quintal	q	100,000	220.46 pounds
kilogram	kg	1,000	2.2046 pounds
hectogram	hg	100	3.527 ounces
dekagram	dag	10	0.353 ounce
gram	g *or* gm	1	0.035 ounce
decigram	dg	0.10	1.543 grains
centigram	cg	0.01	0.154 grain
milligram	mg	0.001	0.015 grain

Metric Conversion Chart

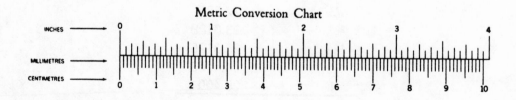

Index